LESBIANISM

LESBIANISM

A Study of
Female Homosexuality

By

DAVID H. ROSEN, M.D.
The University of California School of Medicine
Department of Psychiatry
The Langley Porter Neuropsychiatric Institute
San Francisco, California

With a Foreword by

EVELYN HOOKER, Ph.D.
Clinical Professor of Psychology
Department of Psychiatry
University of California School of Medicine
Los Angeles, California

CHARLES C THOMAS · PUBLISHER
Springfield · Illinois · U.S.A.

Published and Distributed Throughout the World by
CHARLES C THOMAS • PUBLISHER
BANNERSTONE HOUSE
301-327 East Lawrence Avenue, Springfield, Illinois, U.S.A.

© *1974, by* CHARLES C THOMAS • PUBLISHER
ISBN 0-398-02924-5
Library of Congress Catalog Card Number: 73-11067

With THOMAS BOOKS *careful attention is given to all details of manufacturing and design. It is the Publisher's desire to present books that are satisfactory as to their physical qualities and artistic possibilities and appropriate for their particular use.* THOMAS BOOKS *will be true to those laws of quality that assure a good name and good will.*

Printed in the United States of America
A-2

Library of Congress Cataloging in Publication Data

Rosen, David H   1945-
    Lesbianism.

    1. Lesbianism—United States. I. Title.
[DNLM: 1. Homosexuality. 2. Women. WM615
R812L   1973]
HQ76.3.U5R67   301.41'57   73-11067
ISBN 0-398-02924-5

To the twenty-six women who made this book possible.

FOREWORD

THE FUNDAMENTAL QUESTION to which Dr. Rosen addresses himself in this book is a very timely one: Is female homosexuality a psychiatric disorder or a way of life? The book appears at a time when the American Psychiatric Association is engaged in an intense controversy on the issue of whether to delete homosexuality (male and female) from the Diagnostic Manual of Psychiatric Disorders. The author is firmly on the side of those who recommend deletion and uses his review of the literature as well as his own study of twenty-six lesbians to support his position; thus, he joins a distinguished group of psychiatrists and behavioral scientists who believe that the mental health professions should no longer continue to use their power in stigmatizing a large sexual minority and, by doing so, contributing to the social and psychological problems of the individuals involved.

This slim volume is a much needed contribution to the small but increasing number of empirical studies of lesbians, a subject too long ignored by behavioral scientists. Its primary value, in my opinion, resides in the comprehensive critical review of the literature, and in the detailed presentation of the individual case studies. It is rewarding and illuminating to read each individual case study and Adjective Check List analysis. It is good that the author has included not only the group mean profile of the Adjective Check List, but the individual profiles as well. Mean profiles obliterate individual differences. Most striking is the fact that, with one exception, the mean profile is within normal limits; however, the exception, Counseling Readiness, is well above normal limits. The author notes this fact but minimizes it. It is important to note that a high score on Counseling Readiness indicates that the subjects "tend to worry about themselves, feel left out, are unable to enjoy life to the fullest extent and are unduly anxious." However, an examination of the individual profiles indicates that this high mean score is not typical of *all* individuals and therefore does not

vii

characterize the group as a whole. Some individuals, perhaps half, score well within normal limits or below, while the remainder score very high. Hence, the high group mean.

The foregoing observations on Dr. Rosen's data and the conclusions he draws from them lead me to comment not only on his research but on the current state of research on the issue of homosexuality as an alternative life style, or a psychiatric disorder. As scientists-clinicians in the behavioral sciences, we are often caught in the humanist-citizen vs scientist (faithful to the specific data) dilemma. No one who has been privileged to know responsible, reliable, productive, well-functioning homosexuals, and to know the savage, socially repressive measures of which they are victims, can stand aloof from their struggle to shed the shackles and become first-class citizens. But we must find a way to be faithful to both commitments. As I see it, the way, the solution to the dilemma, is to be faithful to the data, not to over-generalize, but to report accurately, and to interpret accurately whatever the data permit or demand. There may be times when we have no scientific data for our humane action. When Pinel ordered the inmates of "insane asylums" in Paris to have their chains unshackled, was there any scientific evidence buttressing his command? No. Only his own humane conscience. But we in the twentieth century, not only have humane considerations, but scientific evidence as well. And what does the scientific evidence in Dr. Rosen's book, and the accumulated body of literature, indicate about the issue of homosexuality as a psychiatric disorder vs. an alternative life style?

In all of the research studies, including Dr. Rosen's, a significant proportion of individuals in the particular sample function extremely well, without evidence of any psychiatric symptoms, but there are also a number of individuals (varying with the sample selected) who show symptoms of neurotic anxiety and other dysfunctional or maladaptive disturbances. What seems clear is that it is not *inherently* a psychiatric disorder (although psychiatric symptoms may be *associated with it in some cases,* just as with heterosexuality) and that it can be, and is, in many instances a healthy life style. The critical question which should be answered by further research is: what variables in personality, developmental history, and the cultural milieu of the individual lead to a healthy vs a non-healthy homosexual pattern of life? Thus, while in complete agreement with Dr. Rosen that homosexuality as a diagnostic category should be deleted from the Psychiatric Manual, I hope that a careful reading of this book will lead other investigators to design studies which will help to answer this question.

EVELYN HOOKER, PH.D.

Clinical Professor of Psychology
Department of Psychiatry
University of California
School of Medicine

PREFACE

I BECAME INTERESTED in the study of female homosexuality while an undergraduate in psychology at the University of California (Berkeley). In 1965 I attended a conference on sexuality sponsored by the then revolutionary (in the sense that it was ahead of its time) Stiles Hall (The University of California, Berkeley campus based Y.M.C.A. organization). It was at this conference at a session on homosexuality that I first met Phyllis Lyon who kindled my interest in this area and who helped tremendously in making this study possible. Prior to that Stiles Hall meeting, I had naïvely thought that homosexuality was synonomous with male homosexuality and I was unaware that there were as many as or more female homosexuals than male homosexuals. The theme of Phyllis Lyon's presentation at that meeting was that female homosexuality is neither an illness nor a psychiatric malady but rather "a way of life."[1] She stated that there are very few studies of nonpatient lesbians and that the whole subject of female homosexuality has been neglected as a research area by a male-dominated psychiatric research effort that has concentrated on male homosexuality. Her initial supposition became the working hypothesis of my research. I worked closely with Phyllis Lyon and the Daughters of Bilitis (the national lesbian organization that she helped to found in 1955) to gather information for this study. The research design guaranteed the anonymity of the 26 subjects but allowed for a detailed study of female homosexuality in a nonpatient population.

At that time (1965), there were only a few related studies reported in the literature: Henry (1948), Kinsey *et al.* (1953), Armon (1960), Cory (1964), and Bene (1965). Since then, ten nonpatient lesbian studies have been reported: Gundlach and

---

1. This same theme is the subject of a book entitled *Lesbian/Woman* which Phyllis Lyon co-authored with Del Martin.

Riess (1968), Freedman (1968), Kenyon (1968 a and b), Hopkins (1969), Kaye (1971), Saghir and Robins (1971), Thompson, McCandless, and Strickland (1971), Loney (1972), Wolff (1972), and Siegelman (1972). I concur with Hopkins' (1969) apt statement that these research studies "have all attempted to take the subject [lesbianism] out of the myth and psychoanalytic theory stages and bring it into the light, to determine whether the many theories, which at times have been based upon knowledge gleaned from male homosexual studies, have any objective, quantifiable basis" (p. 1433). It is hoped that this monograph will serve the same purpose. Part I is a much needed up to date review of the literature, while part II focuses on the lesbian study that I carried out in the late 1960's. Part III contains a discussion of the working hypothesis more fully developed, and priorities for future action and further research are outlined.

DAVID H. ROSEN

ACKNOWLEDGMENTS

INITIALLY I had planned to report the results of my research study as a journal article. However, Dr. J. M. A. Weiss, (Chairman of Psychiatry at the University of Missouri School of Medidine) after critically reviewing the manuscript suggested that I put together a monograph on this subject because of the uniqueness of this research study and because of the general lack of studies reported in the literature. I am very thankful to Dr. Weiss for his support and encouragement. I owe appreciation to Seward Hiltner (Professor of Theology and Personality at the Princeton Theological Seminary) for his early help and honest criticism. I am indebted to Dr. Judd Marmor (Franz Alexander Professor of Psychiatry, University of Southern California) for his assistance in reviewing the monograph. I extend my gratitude to Dr. Evelyn Hooker (Department of Psychiatry, University of California, Los Angeles and past Chairwoman of the National Institute of Mental Health Committee on Homosexuality) for writing such a thoughtful and excellent foreword to the book.

In addition, I wish to thank the following individuals who all helped in making this project and monograph possible: Dr. Leon Epstein (University of California, San Francisco, Department of Psychiatry), Dr. Bernard Diamond (University of California, Berkeley, School of Criminology), Dr. Alfred Auerback (University of California, San Francisco, Department of Psychiatry), Dr. Marion Steele (San Francisco), Dr. Fariborz Amini (University of California, San Francisco, Department of Psychiatry), James Stoll, Douglas Kreider and Chris Asimos (all of San Francisco), and of course Phyllis Lyon (Associate Director National Sex Forum, Glide Foundation, San Francisco) and Del Martin (founding member with Ms. Lyon of the Daughters of Bilitis, San Francisco). I take pleasure in expressing thanks to Dr. Harrison G. Gough and the Consulting Psychologist Press, Inc. for special permission to reproduce the Adjective Check List, definitions of the scales, and copies of the research subjects profiles; for this privilege I am very grateful. I wish to mention the help provided by Lynn Rosen in scoring and interpreting the Adjective Check List profiles. Sincere and special thanks are due Mary Ann Esser for her expert editorial and technical assistance and Leona Magni for her proficient typing skills in preparing the monograph. Last, but not least, I specifically acknowledge and warmly thank my wife, Deborah Voorhees-Rosen, for her assistance and loving support.

D.H.R.

CONTENTS

LESBIANISM

PART I

REVIEW OF THE LITERATURE

". . . . TO DESCRIBE (HOMOSEXUAL) BEHAVIOR AS UNNATURAL IS TO DEPART FROM STRICT ACCURACY. THE ZOOLOGICAL EVIDENCE SHOWS THAT FEMALE MAMMALS FREQUENTLY DISPLAY MASCULINE COITAL BEHAVIOR WHEN CONFRONTED WITH SEXUALLY RECEPTIVE MEMBERS OF THEIR OWN SEX. THIS HAS BEEN OBSERVED IN MORE THAN A DOZEN SPECIES AND UNDOUBTEDLY OCCURS IN MANY OTHERS NOT YET STUDIED . . . . THE PSYCHOLOGICAL MECHANISMS FOR FEMININE SEXUAL BEHAVIOR ARE FOUND IN ALL MALES AND THOSE FOR MASCULINE BEHAVIOR EXIST IN ALL FEMALES. THE SAME STIMULI THAT ELICIT FEMININE COPULATORY REACTIONS IN THE FEMALE WILL, UNDER APPROPRIATE CONDITIONS, PRODUCE SIMILAR REACTIONS IN MANY MALES; AND THE STIMULUS CONFIGURATION EVOKING MASCULINE RESPONSES IN MALES IS THE ONE WHICH MOST EFFECTIVELY CALLS FORTH THESE SAME RESPONSES ON THE PART OF THE FEMALE. HUMAN HOMOSEXUALITY REFLECTS THE ESSENTIAL BISEXUAL CHARACTER OF OUR MAMMALIAN INHERITANCE. THE EXTREME MODIFIABILITY OF MAN'S SEX LIFE MAKES POSSIBLE THE CONVERSION OF THIS ESSENTIAL BISEXUALITY INTO A FORM OF UNISEXUALITY WITH THE RESULT THAT A MEMBER OF THE SAME SEX EVENTUALLY BECOMES THE ONLY ACCEPTABLE STIMULUS TO AROUSAL" (BEACH, 1948) .

3

CHAPTER I

PATIENT - CENTERED AND NONPATIENT - CENTERED STUDIES

THERE ARE FEW studies on female homosexuality, compared to the numerous reports on male homosexuality. Why has the lesbian been so neglected in the psychiatric literature? Is it because the psychiatric profession is male dominated, as noted by Lyon and Martin (1972)? Is it (as postulated by Socarides, 1963) because lesbians are not under as much external pressure to seek psychiatric treatment, because of society's attitude toward female homosexuals, i.e., the more lenient legal and social sanctions? Is the inattention to lesbianism, as well as to female sexuality in general, derived from the overly *phallocentric* culture we live in, as suggested by Horney (1926) and by Jones (1927)? Possibly, as Romm (1965) pointed out, lesbians are less disturbed than their male counterparts and therefore seek psychiatric help less frequently.

PATIENT-CENTERED STUDIES

A classic report by Freud (1948) dealt with a single case and illustrates the flaws inherent in any attempt to generalize from an isolated case. Freud noted that homosexuality in women had "been neglected by psychoanalytic research." He introduced his case study by stating, "The girl was not in any way ill," but later he spoke of "the patient's abnormality and its development." He stated that the parents of the eighteen-year-old girl desired a "cure" for their "nervous and unruly child." Freud, in my opinion unjustly, ascribed the following "masculine traits" to this "beautiful and well developed girl": "sharp features," "acuteness of comprehension," "lucid objectivity," "not dominated by her passion," and she had assumed the "masculine preference for being lover rather than beloved." Rather dogmatically, Freud stated, "It is always possible by analysis to recognize the causation with certainty." This patient's "analysis showed that the girl suffered from childhood from a strongly marked 'masculine complex'." The primary factors in the case were the patient's "strong mother fixation" coupled with "her mother's indifference" and the patient's "pronounced envy of the penis" of her slightly older brother (this penis envy apparently originated when the patient compared genitals with her brother at about the age of five).

Despite this compact analysis, Freud left the question of etiology open, stating, "The mystery of homosexuality is therefore by no means so simple as it is commonly depicted in popular expositions" (p. 230). Further, "Psychoanalysis has a common basis with biology, in that it presupposes an original bisexuality in human beings (as in animals)" (p. 231). "It is not for psychoanalysis to solve the problem of homosexuality. It must rest content with disclosing the psychical mechanisms that resulted in determination of the object-choice, and with tracing the paths leading from them to the instinctual basis of the disposition. There its work ends, and it leaves the rest to biological research" (p. 230).

Ernest Jones (1927), from his experience of analyzing simultaneously five cases of overt female homosexuality, felt it could be traced back to two critical factors, an extreme oral erotism and a very strong sadism. Jones felt that the lesbian has a strong infantile fixation on the mother (connected with the oral stage) and this is always succeeded by a very strong father fixation.

De Saussure's monograph in 1929 was the first written on female homosexuality. He concluded that his patients identified with their fathers and were unable to accept their womanhood because of "penis envy." In 1932, Deutsch published a paper, "On female homosexuality," that was considered for many years to be "the most important article on the subject." Her study was "based on the experience gained from the more or less profound analysis of eleven cases of female homosexuality." Deutsch considered lesbianism to be a "perversion" involving "a mother fixation" (murderous rage and hate for the mother which is transformed into love for the mother substituted in love relationships with other women), "the castration complex," "penis envy," and the assumption of a "masculine identification" as a reaction to being disappointed by a passive father. In summation, she considered female homosexuality to be a renunciation of the father and a definite persistence of the mother attachment. Deutsch and Freud both held the view that "the homosexual woman reproduces the mother-child relationship (Freud, 1933, p. 178).

Rado (1933) believed that the female is basically masochistic and wishes to be violated in sex. As a reaction to fears of mutilation and destruction by pregnancy and childbirth some women "escape" into homosexuality. Fenichel (1945) believed that two etiological factors are crucial with regard to female homosexuality: castration complex and subsequent repulsion from heterosexuality, and an attraction for females through an early fixation on the mother. Bergler (1951) considered an aggressive hatred for the dominating mother, warded off by a libidinous feeling, to be of etiological significance in female homosexuality.

Caprio (1954) presented a good historical perspective of lesbianism from the time of antiquity to 1954. However, the bulk of his book dealt with his own "clinical observations" from his psychotherapeutic work with lesbians. He considered female homosexuality to be a symptom of a "deep seated unresolved neurosis," and rejected various psychogenetic theories and psychoanalytic theories in order to regard narcissism as a primary drive and lesbianism as "an extension of autoeroticism cooperative masturbation." He considered lesbians to be doomed to "unhappiness" because of the impermanence of their sexual relationships and their numerous neurotic complaints. Caprio stated, "Our modern attitude should be one of understanding—regarding homosexuality as an illness in the sense that it represents a form of sexual immaturity—frustration and loneliness" (p. 40).

Bacon (1956) stressed the regression to a maternal-child relationship after giving up the attachment to the father. The patient is unable to seek out another male because of "fear of retaliation on the father's part."

Many other lesbian causation theories, concepts related to fears and other causal factors, have been noted by Romm (1965), Wilbur (1965), and Lyon and Martin (1972). Some of these

are: fear of growing up and assuming adult responsibilities; fear
of dominance and destruction; fear of rejection; fear of the
opposite sex; fear of castration and of the penis; the desire to
conquer and possess the mother; neurotic dependency; heterosexual trauma (including rape) ; seduction in adolescence by an
older female; first sexual experience with someone of the same
sex and finding it pleasurable; tomboy behavior in early childhood; prolonged absence of the mother; masturbation with a re-
sulting clitoral fixation; social factors (such as heterosexual
taboos and unisexual, all female, groups) ; and physical factors
(genetic, constitutional, and endocrine abnormalities) .[2] Cory
(1964) suggested that we must look further for a comprehensive
theory. He thought lesbianism is a learned condition, a phenome-
non with many causes, including psychological and sociological
ones.

Unfortunately, one of the finest books on homosexuality,
edited by Marmor (1965) , deals primarily with male homosexuality, with only two chapters devoted to female homosexuality.
Marmor, too, stressed the multifactorial causality of homosexuality and stated that "no single constellation of factors . . . can
adequately explain all homosexual deviations. The simple fact is
that dominating and seductive mothers; weak, hostile, or detached
fathers; and the multiple variations on these themes . . . cannot
. . . be *in themselves* specific causative factors" (p. 5) . In contrast
to Marmor's clear message of warning regarding simplistic
theories, Wilbur (1965) outlined the following theory: "In the
triangular constellation of the father-mother-homosexual daughter
we generally find a father who tends to be passive, unassertive,
gentle, and detached; a mother who is dominant, domineering,
guilt-inducing, and hostile; and a daughter who is hostile toward
her mother, who cannot turn to her father because of what she
perceives as his weakness, and who suffers from severe feelings of

2. Perloff (1965) has reviewed numerous endocrine investigations that have produced no conclusive findings regarding hormonal imbalance as an etiological
   factor. However, a recent report of hormone imbalance in lesbians warrants
   further study (Loraine *et al.*, 1971). No definite constitutional or genetic factors have been found to be of etiological significance with regard to lesbianism
   (Marmor, 1965, pp. 6-9) .

rejection and longing" (p. 276). She went on to state: "Female homosexual relationships are characterized by great ambivalence, by great longing for love, by intense elements of hostility, and by the presence of chronic anxiety. These relationships are unstable and often transient. They do not contribute to the individual's need for stability and love" (pp. 280-81).

Romm (1965) also made some simplistic, generalized, and pejorative statements: "Homosexuals of both sexes are human beings who have given up hope of ever being accepted by their parents and by the society in which they live. They are basically unhappy because normal family life with the fulfillment in having children can never be within their reach. The label *gay* behind which they hide is a defense mechanism against the emptiness, the coldness, and the futility of their lives" (p. 291). "Female homosexuality is a psychosexual aberration. It is an unfortunate result of the early impact of a stressful environment upon an individual who, for reasons not yet fully understood, is unable to handle the ensuing anxiety connected with heterosexuality. As a compromise, such a person may take refuge in an erotic relationship with a member of her own sex" (p. 298). Both Romm and Wilbur apparently were writing about homosexual patients and not about the majority of female homosexuals who are functioning and well adjusted nonpatients.

Kaye *et al.* (1967) studied 24 female homosexual patients who were in psychoanalysis, concluding that "homosexuality in women, rather than being a conscious volitional preference, is a massive adaptational response to a crippling inhibition of normal heterosexual development" (p. 633). They claimed that the etiology of lesbianism is associated with castration fear and a fear of pregnancy. They went so far as to outline the following "early prodromata" that should "alert parents and family physicians" to potential lesbians: seeking physical fights in childhood, dislike of and play less with dolls, trend toward excessive play with guns, preference for boys' games and a tendency not to play house, tendency to see themselves as tomboys, and the development of strong crushes on women during puberty.

NONPATIENT-CENTERED STUDIES

All of the investigators mentioned above (except Cory and
Lyon and Martin) gathered their information from clinical
studies of lesbian patients and not from women who were lesbians
but not patients. Henry's thorough study of homosexuality (1948)
included 40 "homosexual" women and represents one of the first
attempts to "state facts without personal bias." He considered
lesbianism to be a form of sexual variance, a "by-product of
civilization," and stressed the contributing factors of constitutional deficiencies, family patterns of sexual adjustment, and the lack
of opportunity for psychosexual development. Henry considered
lesbianism to be a medical and social problem rather than a legal
one.

Kinsey *et al.* (1953) were the first to investigate "normal"
women nonpatients (including some homosexuals) regarding
their sexual behavior. This pioneering research provided the first
glimpse into homosexuality[3] as natural sexual behavior rather
than as psychiatric illness. The research findings were summarized
as follows. "The data indicate that the factors leading to homosexual behavior are 1) the basic physiologic capacity of every
mammal to respond to any sufficient stimulus; 2) the accident
which leads an individual into his or her first sexual experience
with a person of the same sex; 3) the conditioning effects of such
experience; and 4) the indirect but powerful conditioning which
the opinions of other persons and the social codes may have on
an individual's decision to accept or reject this type of sexual
contact" (p. 447).

Armon's (1960) innovative study of nonpatient lesbians tested
all the major psychoanalytic theories by utilizing psychological
projective techniques (Rorschach and Figure Drawing). It was

3. *Kinsey's sexual behavioral rating scale*
    0 = Completely heterosexual
    1 = Primarily heterosexual (little homosexual experience and drive)
    2 = Predominantly heterosexual (considerable homosexual experience and drive)
    3 = Relatively bisexual in experience and drive.
    4 = Predominantly homosexual (considerable heterosexual experience and drive)
    5 = Primarily homosexual (little heterosexual experience and drive)
    6 = Completely homosexual

hypothesized that homosexual women would be rated higher in such characteristics as (1) dependency; (2) hostile-fearful conception of the feminine role; (3) disparagement of men; (4) hostile-fearful conception of the masculine role; (5) confusion and conflict in sexual identification; and (6) limited personal-social relations. It was concluded that the majority of lesbians cannot be distinguished from heterosexuals on the basis of projective test performance. The hypothesis that obtained the strongest support was (2) hostile-fearful conception of the feminine role. Armon stated, "This finding would tend to support the concept of [lesbianism] as a defense against hostility, fear, and guilt in relation to women (presumably originating in significant early relationships)" (p. 307). She concluded that "the failure to find many clear-cut differences which are consistent for the majority of the group would suggest that homosexuality is not a clinical entity" (p. 308).

Bene (1965) tested numerous psychoanalytic theories by comparing relevant childhood recollections of lesbians with those of married women. The lesbians were "more often hostile towards and afraid of their fathers than were the married women, and they felt more often that their fathers were weak and incompetent" (p. 821). Bene further stated, "The results also point towards a relationship between the parents' wish for a son and the homosexuality of their daughter" (p. 821).

Kenyon (1968a) studied a nonclinical group of English lesbians and concluded that they were higher in neuroticism than a comparison group of heterosexuals. However, he was careful to state that "the exact nature of this association needs further study to see whether lesbianism is but one facet of a general emotional instability or whether lesbianism itself and society's reactions to it have produced a secondary emotional reaction" (p. 512).

Hopkins (1969) utilized psychological testing to carry out a study of 24 nonpatient lesbians matched with a control group of 24 heterosexual women. Her findings were the opposite of Kenyon's and she stated, "The traditionally applied *neurotic* label is not necessarily applicable [to the lesbian group]" (p. 1436). She concluded, "The following terms are suggested as appropriately descriptive of the lesbian personality in comparison to her heterosexual female counterpart: 1) more independent, 2) more resilient, 3) more reserved, 4) more dominant, 5) more bohemian, 6) more self-sufficient and 7) more composed" (p. 1436).

Freedman (1968) gave a battery of psychological tests to a sample of lesbians and to a heterosexual control group and found that there were no differences between the two groups in a "global measure of psychological adjustment." He found that "the members of the [lesbian] group were no more neurotic than the members of the control group" and that homosexuality is not necessarily related to psychological disturbance. He stated, "Hopefully, behavioral scientists will become more aware of studies like this on the psychological concomitants of homosexuality and will change their theoretical assumptions and personal attitudes on this topic as consequence" (p. 3) .

Kaye (1971) studied 157 nonpatient lesbians and found the "close-binding, intimate father" to be the etiological counterpart to the "close-binding mother" found in studies of male homosexuality. He also concluded that all the lesbians were bisexual and treatable, that is, they could be reoriented to exclusive heterosexuality.

Saghir and Robins (1971) studied 57 nonpatient lesbians matched with controls and found that "there was no significant difference in the prevalence of neurotic disorders" between homosexual females and matched controls (p. 510) . However, they did find that the lesbians had "more depressions, suicide attempts and usually abused alcohol more often [than their heterosexual controls]" (p. 510) . Still, they concluded, "The majority of [lesbians] functioned adequately and were productive with no significant disabilities" (p. 510) .

Thompson, McCandless, and Strickland (1971) studied 84 nonpatient lesbians, matched with controls, utilizing the Adjective Check List and the Semantic Differential Test. They found "no important difference" between the two groups. The only significant difference between the two groups was that the lesbians were rated higher on the Adjective Check List scale that measures self-confidence.

Loney (1972) studied 11 nonpatient, self-labelled lesbians by means of a questionnaire and the Family Adjustment Test, utilizing 12 heterosexual women for controls. She found that the majority of the homosexual women were "married" to other women, that is, were involved in healthy continuing interpersonal relationships. She felt "this finding might be used to buttress the rather frequent contention that homosexual women are less 'neurotic' and more 'socialized' than homosexual men" (p. 62), as found by Gundlach (1969). Siegelman (1972) studied 84 nonpatient homosexual women and contrasted the results of psychological tests with those of heterosexual women controls. Siegelman found the lesbians to have higher scores on tendermindedness and lower scores on depression, submission, and anxiety. His failure to find female homosexuals more neurotic than female heterosexuals agrees with the reported findings of Armon (1960), Freedman (1968), Hopkins (1969), and Thompson, McCandless, and Strickland (1971). Siegelman stated that "the lesbians are better adjusted in some respects than the heterosexuals, as has also been reported by Freedman (1968) and by Hopkins (1969)" (p. 479). He stated further, "The psychoanalytic contention that [lesbians] have high dependency needs (Fenichel, 1945) was not supported by Armon (1960) or by the present study, and strong independent tendencies have been found by Hopkins (1969)" (p. 480).

The results of Siegelman's study, together with the findings of Freedman (1968) and of Hopkins (1969) directly contradict the contention of Socarides (1968), Caprio (1954), Romm (1965), Wilbur (1965), and Kaye *et al.* (1967) that lesbians have a deep sense of inferiority. Siegelman concluded, "The need to sample a wider segment of the homosexual community is emphasized . . . An absence of differences in homosexual versus heterosexual adjustment is reported in most studies using non-clinical subjects. On the other hand, the writing of psychiatrists describing their patients, typically reflects the belief that homosexuals are seriously maladjusted . . . Additional studies with longer, more representative samples and diverse methodologies must be conducted for a more adequate evaluation of this result" (p. 480).

PART II

A LESBIAN RESEARCH STUDY

"WHY SHOULDN'T WE BE LOVERS? I WOULDN'T SUDDENLY BEGIN TO LET YOU TAKE ME OVER AND DO YOUR BIDDING. I WOULDN'T TRY TO MODEL MYSELF AFTER YOU. I COULD HAVE LOVING AND INDEPENDENCE TOO. I WOULDN'T BE AFRAID OF BEING LEFT, OR FEEL JEALOUS IF YOU WERE WITH SOMEONE ELSE. I'D BE MORE SECURE IN OUR FRIENDSHIP KNOWING THAT WE WERE TOUCHING EACH OTHER BECAUSE WE LIKE EACH OTHER. THERE'S PLENTY OF LOVING TO BE MADE IN THE WORLD — NO NEED TO FEAR FOR WHERE THE NEXT GOOD TIME IS COMING FROM. WHY SHOULDN'T WE? NOT BECAUSE WE HATE MEN, BUT BECAUSE WE LOVE OURSELVES.

"THERE WILL BE TIMES IN OUR LIVES WHEN WE WILL FEEL MORE SEXUAL RAPPORT WITH WOMEN; WHEN WE'RE WORKING WITH THEM OR LIVING WITH THEM, OR LOVING THEM. SOMETIMES THAT CHOICE SPRINGS FROM FEAR OF MEN. FEARS OF RAPE, OF POWERLESSNESS, OF HUMILIATION ARE COMMON AND IN OUR CULTURE SUCH EXPECTATIONS ARE REALISTIC. AN INCREDIBLE NUMBER OF WOMEN—INCLUDING MIDDLE-CLASS WELL-PRO-TECTED WOMEN—HAVE HAD HORRIFYING EXPERIENCES OF SEXUAL ABUSE. OUT OF FIFTEEN WOMEN WHO DISCUSSED THE TOPIC RECENTLY, FOUR HAD BEEN RAPED.

"FRIGIDITY WITH MEN, OR A TURN TOWARD FEMALE LOVERS IS NOT SURPRISING WHEN THE SOCIALLY ACCEPTABLE HETEROSEXUAL ENCOUN-TERS HAVE BEEN SO DESTRUCTIVE. PSYCHOLOGISTS CALL THIS ABNORMAL. FEAR OF MEN, THEY SAY, IS ABNORMAL. WE SAY, EACH OF US WILL HAVE TO DRAW OUR OWN CONCLUSIONS, AND DEAL WITH OUR OWN FEARS. FOR SOME THIS MAY MEAN GETTING OUR BODIES IN SHAPE SO THAT WE CAN FIGHT WITH MEN ON THEIR OWN TERMS. FOR OTHERS, IT JUST MEANS CHOOSING THE RIGHT MALE LOVERS. AND SOME OF US MAY JUST DECIDE TO CHUCK THE WHOLE THING AND EXPRESS OUR LOVE AND SEXUALITY WITH EACH OTHER. IT MAY BE THAT WHAT WE NEED TO DO IN ORDER TO MAINTAIN OUR INTEGRITY AS HUMAN BEINGS IS TO MOVE FREELY THROUGH

15

THESE AND OTHER CHOICES GIVEN THE CIRCUMSTANCES OF OUR LIVES AT
ANY PARTICULAR TIME, AND NOT BE BOUND BY MYTHS AND TABOOS THAT
KEEP US FROM DOING WHAT IS RIGHT FOR US AT EACH MOMENT" ("AN
OPEN LETTER TO MY SISTERS" FROM *Our Bodies, Ourselves,* 1973) .

CHAPTER II

GENERAL CORRELATIONS

INTRODUCTION

T HIS STUDY ATTEMPTED to gain insight into and understanding of the female homosexual, defined as a woman who is motivated, in adult life, by a primary erotic, psychological, emotional, and social attraction to and interest in other women. The study was planned to be essentially descriptive, that is, to assess the characteristics of lesbianism, and the research method involved a phenomenological approach, offering the lesbians' own self-referent statements about how they became homosexuals. The study employed an exploratory design and the information was procured by an extensive questionnaire (Appendix I) and by follow-up telephone interviews when necessary. Gough's "Adjective Check List" (Appendix II) was utilized to gather additional information. The primary purpose was twofold: (1) to test and develop the working hypothesis that female homosexuality is not an illness but "a way of life" and (2) to formulate problems for more precise investigation and establish priorities for future action and further research.

The 26 subjects were volunteers and exhibit a selective bias since all were members of the Daughters of Bilitis (a national homophile organization based in San Francisco). All information was coded. The subjects were identified by the letters A through Z for the sake of anonymity. Data were tabulated, correlated, and summated. Individual case descriptions emphasized both contributing factors of etiology and psychological and social adjustment as seen by the lesbians themselves.

QUESTIONNAIRE DATA

The questionnaire (Appendix I) was designed to obtain general personal and social data, information about sexual history and personal and social adjustment, and statements about what life experiences were etiologically significant. Questions were also asked about how satisfied the subjects were as lesbians and whether or not they would change if they could relive their lives.

The questionnaire, along with the Adjective Check List, was distributed in sealed packets by the Daughters of Bilitis organization to 26 of their members who had volunteered. The subjects returned the completed questionnaires and Adjective Check Lists by return mail. They included their telephone numbers so they could be reached if necessary to clarify answers or to obtain further information (it was only necessary to contact four subjects by telephone).

The answers to questions of a general nature have been summarized and are reported in this section. Answers to questions of a more individual nature (Numbers 16, 17, 18, 19, 20, 31, 33, and 34) are reported in Chapter 3 (The Individual Cases). The results of two questions (Numbers 6 and 13) were not included because they were judged to be of little importance.

1. Occupation

The occupations of the sample group varied widely. There were ten secretaries, a teacher, a nurse, a clerk, a kennel owner, and an electronic engineer, among the occupations listed.

2. Marital Status

All 26 women were single. Twenty had never been married, four were divorced or separated, one had an annulled marriage, and one was widowed. The four divorced or separated all had children, one woman having adopted hers. Five outside of the previously married group stated they would like to have children in the future but only two felt that they would do so.

3. Age

The group ranged in age from twenty to forty-nine years, the average age being thirty-four years.

4. Educational Background

All but one of the 26 subjects had been graduated from high school. The one exception went as far as the eleventh grade. Twenty-four attended college; eight obtained bachelor degrees, one received a master's degree, one received a law degree.

5. Religion

Twelve women of the 26 stated they had no religion at all. The rest varied as follows: three Lutheran (one attended regularly), three Catholic (two attended regularly), two Unitarian, two Jewish, one Protestant, one Methodist, one Baptist, and one who called herself a "metaphysicist."

7. In your childhood were you closer to your father or mother?

Twenty of the 26 felt closer to their mothers during their formative years. Of the remaining six, four felt closer to their fathers while two felt close to neither parent.

8. If you had to pick one parent as the one you liked best which would you pick, father or mother?

Seventeen picked their mother as the parent they liked best and six picked their father. Three liked both parents equally. (It is interesting to note that three of the women who felt closest to their mother during their childhood years stated they liked their fathers the best.)

9. Description of fathers

29. Characterization of men in general

Fathers:

15 dominant	14 warm	16 kind	15 loving
7 weak	8 cold	7 punitive	8 not loving
4 neither dominant nor weak	4 neither warm nor cold	3 neither kind nor punitive	3 neither loving nor not loving

Other traits attributed to the fathers were uncommunicative, bastard, passive, gentle, quiet, alcoholic, and reserved.

Men in general:

14 dominant	11 cold	14 punitive	13 not loving
5 weak	9 warm	8 kind	9 loving
7 neither	6 neither	4 neither	4 neither

The fathers for the most part were perceived to be dominant, warm, kind, and loving, whereas men in general were described as dominant, cold, punitive, and not loving.

10. Description of mothers
30. Characterization of women in general

Mothers:

17 dominant	15 warm	14 kind	17 loving
7 weak	9 cold	9 punitive	6 not loving
2 neither	2 neither	3 neither	3 neither

Women in general:

9 dominant	19 warm	19 kind	20 loving
7 weak	2 cold	0 punitive	1 not loving
10 neither	5 neither	7 neither	5 neither

Women in general were described as being like the mothers (but more so) —dominant, warm, kind, and loving. This is noteworthy since most of the women in the sample described men in general as being dominant, cold, punitive, and not loving.

11, 12, and 14 (Concerned with the parents' attitudes toward sex, and with whom the women in the sample grew up)

All of the parents expressed little affection for each other in the home. Most were not well adjusted to each other in their sexual relations. Some of the fathers molested their daughters; one stepfather raped his daughter, and another attempted rape. In all the homes there was *no* discussion or mention of sex. Nineteen of the women grew up with both parents, four grew up with their mothers, and three grew up with the mother and stepfather.

15. Do your parents know you are a lesbian?

Eight of the 26 reported that their parents know that they are lesbians. Sixteen stated that their parents did not know and two said they did not know whether their parents know.

21, 22, 23, and 28. (Concerning bisexuality, first sexual experience (male or female), whether or not they have ever had sexual intercourse with a male, and whether they are attracted to men sexually or as friends)

Eight women out of the 26 had never experienced sexual intercourse with a man. However, one of these eight was attracted sexually to men. Of the 18 women who had experienced sexual intercourse with a man, three were bisexual (the only bisexual women of the whole sample) and stated they were sexually attracted to men. Three others, though they were not bisexual, were attracted to men sexually. Ten were attracted to men as friends, and two were not attracted to men at all. Sixteen women reported having their first sexual experience with a woman while 10 experienced their first sexual relationship with a man.

24. How do you see yourself, masculine or feminine?

How do you think others see you, masculine or feminine?

The average for 14 of the women who saw themselves as feminine was Feminine—6 (see question #24 in questionnaire, Appendix I). The average for the other twelve who saw themselves as masculine was Masculine—4. These two groups only differed by one point in the masculine-feminine rating scale and neither group was near the extreme end of the scale. (This compares fairly well with the Adjective Check List results wherein 15 saw themselves as feminine, seven as masculine, and four as neither.) Nineteen thought that others saw them as feminine, the average being Feminine—6. The other seven thought others perceived them as masculine. This averaged out to be Masculine—4.

25. Roles played in sexual intercourse

Thirteen of the 26 women played both *masculine* and *feminine* roles. Nine of the remaining 13 played a *masculine* or active role in the sexual act whereas four played a strictly *feminine* or passive role.

26. How the group as a whole felt about lesbianism.

Twenty felt that lesbianism is good (morally), healthy (psychologically), and satisfying (physically). One felt it is bad (morally), unhealthy (psychologically), yet satisfying (physically). Another felt it is bad, unhealthy, and unsatisfying, while still another stated it is good, satisfying, but that the question concerning 'healthy or unhealthy psychologically' was unfair. She added, "Most lesbians are psychologically disturbed, but not because they are lesbians. The state of lesbianism cannot be said to be either psychologically healthy or unhealthy. If the lesbian is psychologically adjusted in other facets of her personality, the state of lesbianism is healthy. But, in many cases the lesbian becomes a lesbian because of other psychological disorders, of which her lesbianism is only one manifestation. Of course, psychological disorders are not healthy when they inhibit the adjustment of the individual." Three others refused to answer the question at all.

27. a) How do you meet other lesbians?

Fifteen of the 26 stated they usually meet other lesbians at "gay" bars or "gay parties." Twelve said they meet lesbians at the Daughters of Bilitis. Seven are introduced to lesbians by friends while six said they meet them sometimes at work. (There is overlap here, for example, one woman might have met lesbians at the Daughters of Bilitis, at "gay" bars, and at work.)

    b) What cues do you use in deciding whether or not to approach a woman?

Fifteen stated they never *approached* other women. Ten said they did *approach* women using the following cues:

2 *Eye conversation* or eye contact
2 *Butch* or masculine appearance, short hair, tailored clothes, man's watch, etc.
2 Attractive feminine characteristics
1 If smiled at by another woman in a particular manner
3 By starting conversations

    c) What physical characteristics are important to you in a woman sexual partner?

The following were the most important (mentioned the highest number of times) :

12 Feminine characteristics (attractive, good figure, natural, beautiful)
8 Cleanliness
6 Neatness
5 Masculine characteristics (handsome, mannish women, flat chested, short hair)

    d) What characteristics are important to you regarding a woman as a long-term companion?

The following were the most important (mentioned the highest number of times) :

12 Understanding   12 Intelligence
9 Honesty-Loyalty   9 Kindness-Tenderness
8 Warmness   8 Sense of humor
6 Emotional stability   5 Sense of independence

5 Maturity

4 Spiritual or religious

2 Cleanliness

2 Responsible

4 Sensitivity

2 Not narcissistic

2 Tolerant

2 Dependable

1 "A partner who will care for my children and me"

The following example will give the reader an idea of how this question was answered: "As a long-term companion, which is the only type I have ever sought, the following are important: first of all, that she be healthy-minded, religious, intelligent, tolerant, stable, dependable, trustworthy, honest, understanding, gentle, not-narcissistic, not overly-glamorous, (perhaps all of these things could fall under one word: mature) ."

32. If you could relive your life, and if you had a choice, would you become a lesbian? Why or why not?

Fourteen out of the sample stated that they would become lesbians again if they could relive their lives. Their reasons were varied and included the following:

"Cannot imagine it otherwise." "I've been very happy and healthy." "This life is safe and satisfying. I don't like children and firmly believe that family life destroys the inborn artist and creative powers within a person." "I like (basically) the person I am." "Satisfied with being bisexual." "Yes—despite much loneliness and frustration." "I can have a deeper understanding of human nature (spanning both sexes). It has kept me from being complacent and intolerant."

Nine maintained that if given another chance at life they would not become lesbians. Their reasons varied and included the following:

"Too much unhappiness and loneliness." "I would prefer a life more stable and more socially and religiously acceptable." "Bothered unduly by being *different* and *outside*." "Heterosexual life is usually simpler." "If I had a choice I would not be a woman at all, I would be a man. Men have more freedom and opportunities." "I am not really fulfilled." "In today's society it is very hard to be a lesbian as it is not yet accepted. Many lesbians become quite confused because they find it hard to adjust to the demands of the society. When lesbianism does become acceptable as a normal outlet, your question would have to read 'If you could relive your life, would you choose to love or not to love?'." "It is too difficult to fulfill one's varied needs in life as a lesbian. But more even than this, I think, I recall the many emotional agonies I have undergone, and which I still undergo, constituting a feeling of loneliness and impossibility to the whole scheme of things. I never would choose such agonies again. Probably it is basically the knowledge that I do not seem to fit into things—I neither fit into the world of men, nor do I fit into that of women—I land somewhere in between with all my feelings and desires and so neither side understands me or cares one way or another. It is only my religion (Roman Catholic) that has kept me safe and sane, as far as I can see, and kept me from despondency such as some feel in this regard. For I trust in the goodness of God and therefore in the goodness of my own nature. It is only what I do with it or do not do with it, and the constant temptations and uncertainties, which cause me much unhappiness. The one big question is: how am I to satisfy the most basic of human needs? The love of one particular person, the close relationship? Both are closed to me: the male because I *cannot* establish such a relationship, and the female because I *must not* establish such a relationship. This is the true quandary of every homosexual, whether or not she or he admits it."

One woman stated that she did not know, while two others chose not to answer the question at all.

ADJECTIVE CHECK LIST

The Adjective Check List (Appendix II) was chosen because it is simple to administer and it allows persons to describe themselves in a direct and straightforward manner. It also fit well with the phenomenological research design. The Adjective Check List has been widely employed and it has been found to be useful as an indicator of self-concept, self-esteem, and personal adjustment. The general results of the Adjective Check List are reported in this section. The individual results are discussed in Chapter 3 (The Individual Cases) and the individual profiles are included as Appendix III. Both the general and the individual Adjective Check List profiles were scored (high scores = above norm of 60 and low scores = below norm of 40), and interpreted by using *The Adjective Check List Manual* (Gough and Heilbrun, 1965).

The Adjective Check List profile for the sample as a whole (the mean was calculated from the total score on each scale, and then profiled) falls within the normal range on every scale except the Counseling Readiness (Crs) scale (Fig. 1). The relatively high score (61) in Crs can be interpreted to mean that the women in the group as a whole tend to worry about themselves, they feel left out, unable to enjoy life to its fullest extent, and are unduly anxious.

The adjectives most frequently checked and not checked are reproduced in tabular form (Table I). The adjectives are listed along with the percentage of the total group that checked the respective adjectives.

There is an interesting relationship between the characteristics ascribed to the women the lesbians are searching for as long-term companions (as described in the questionnaire) and the self-descriptive adjectives most frequently checked on the Adjective Check List. Understanding and intelligence showed the highest correlation, while honesty-loyalty, kindness, warmness, humorousness, stability, sensitivity, independence, and maturity followed.

PROFILE SHEET FOR THE ADJECTIVE CHECK LIST

Name _____ Figure 1. The Sample of the twenty-six women as a group. _____ Age _____ Date _____ May 1956.

Sex (circle one) M F   Other Information _____ The mean scores are represented here.

	No Ckd	Df	Fav	Un-Fav	S-Cfd	S-Cn	Lab	Per Adj	Ach	Dom	End	Ord	Int	Nur	Aff	Het	Exh	Aut	Agg	Cha	Suc	Aba	Def	Crs
T	58	43	50	52	51	50	54	46	50	47	48	50	52	46	42	48	51	56	54	52	52	49	44	61
Raw																								

Standard Scores

C Norm Table

TABLE I
THE MOST FREQUENTLY CHECKED ADJECTIVES BY THE GROUP AS A WHOLE

Adjectives checked 18 times by 69% of the total sample of 26 lesbians:

civilized	sentimental
conscientious	sociable
enthusiastic	soft-hearted
good natured	stubborn
healthy	unconventional
informal	warm
independent	

Adjectives checked 19 times by 73% of the sample:

adventurous	impulsive
considerate	individualistic
discreet	logical
forgiving	natural
helpful	reasonable

Adjectives checked 20 times by 77% of the sample:

adaptable	gentle
affectionate	generous
alert	kind
appreciative	practical
dependable	reasonable
curious	responsible
fair-minded	serious
idealistic	sincere
honest	stable

Adjectives checked 21 times by 81% of the sample:

cooperative	logical
emotional	rational
imaginative	reflective
humorous	reliable

Adjectives checked 23 times by 88% of the sample:

interests wide	understanding

Adjectives checked 24 times by 92% of the sample:

capable	sensitive
intelligent	

THE MOST INFREQUENTLY CHECKED ADJECTIVES BY THE GROUP AS A WHOLE

Adjectives checked 0 times by 0% of the sample:

affected	shallow
blustery	unintelligent
cruel	unemotional
hard-hearted	

Table I

Adjectives checked 1 time by 3.84% of the sample:

arrogant	smug
infantile	stingy
obnoxious	superstitious
prudish	thankless
quarrelsome	undependable
rude	unexcitable
shiftless	unfriendly
sly	unkind
whiny	

Adjectives checked 2 times by 7.7% of the sample:

apathetic	meek
autocratic	rattlebrained
cold	rigid
commonplace	slow
despondent	spineless
fickle	sulky
gloomy	timid
handsome	tough
indifferent	unscrupulous
interests narrow	vindictive
intolerant	

CHAPTER III

THE INDIVIDUAL CASES

THE LESBIAN walks unnoticed in our society. Those described in this study included a teacher, an engineer, a baby-sitter, a nurse, a clerk, and several secretaries. They were single and ranged in age from twenty to forty-nine years. Their educational level was high (24 of the 26 attended college). The lesbian is represented in the three major religions, Catholic, Jewish, and Protestant, yet nearly one-half of this sample had no religion. In childhood they generally felt closer to their mothers than their fathers. They mostly described their mothers as dominant, warm, kind, and loving, and women in general as being like the mothers, but even more so, except they were seen as neither dominant nor weak. The fathers for the most part were perceived to be dominant, warm, kind, and loving, whereas men in general were depicted as being dominant, cold, punitive, and not-loving. These lesbians' first sexual experiences were either "unsatisfying" with males or "satisfying" with females. Ten of the 26 had their first sexual experience with males and generally depicted them as "indifferent" and "disappointing." Eleven of the 16 who experienced sex first with a female described their experience as "wonderful," and "satisfying." The majority grew up with both parents. In all the homes there was no discussion or mention of sex. Most of the parents expressed little affection for each other and were not well adjusted in their sexual relations. Overall, these lesbians felt that female homosexuality was good (morally), healthy (psychologically), and satisfying (physically). More than half the sample maintained that they would become lesbians again if they could relive their lives.

The cause of female homosexuality as the lesbians themselves understood it involved a complexity of variables. A concluding crystallized statement on the causation of lesbianism was not the purpose of this study. Each of these subjects had her own unique causal pattern, and individuality in etiology that can be appreciated in the summation contained in Tables II and III.

TABLE II
CONTRIBUTING CAUSAL FACTORS

Let-ter	Type of Sexual Role; Masculine, Feminine or (Both): Bisexual	Parents	Contributing Factors in Causation
A	Feminine Bisexual	Father: died when *A* was 8 years old Mother: weak	1. Trauma of father's death 2. A cruel brother, pseudo father, who was sadistic
B	Feminine Bisexual	Step-father: dominant, cold, punitive, not-loving Mother: dominant, warm, punitive, loving	1. Trauma 2. Raped by step-father at 8 years of age
C	Feminine	Father: weak, cold, not-loving, alcoholic Mother: dominant, cold, punitive, not loving (psychotic)	1. Seduction by lesbian
D	Sees self masculine, but feels others see her as feminine. Both roles in sexual relations	Father: kind, warm, loving Mother: dominant, cold, punitive, seductive	1. Attachment to mother and resentful of brother's favorite place. 2. Broken home
E	Sees self feminine, and feels others see her as feminine. Both roles in sexual relations	Father: weak, warm, loving Mother: dominant, cold, not-loving	1. Unstable home 2. First sexual experience— seduced by brother-in-law at age 13 3. "Didn't outgrow infantile desire for close physical contact with mother."
F	Feminine	Father: dominant, cold, kind, loving Mother: weak, cold, kind, not-loving	1. "Oldest of four children (also being a woman)"
G	Masculine	Father: dominant, cold, kind, loving Mother: weak, cold, kind, loving	1. "Fear of Pregnancy" (first sexual experience with male— "disappointed and pregnant") 2. "Never wanted to be married" 3. "Feeling of protective-ness and warmth with women"

TABLE II
CONTRIBUTING CAUSAL FACTORS—(Continued)

Letter	Type of Sexual Role; Masculine, Feminine or (Both): Bisexual	Parents	Contributing Factors in Causation
H	Masculine	Father: dominant, kind Mother: dominant, punitive	1. First sexual experience with female—"Satisfied" (Never had sex with male) 2. "Always wanted older sisters (was an only child) made imaginary sisters" 3. "Crushes on females in school during adolescence"
I	Feminine	"Good-home, normal, middle-class family"	1. "Oldest of four children, had more responsibility" 2. "I can remember 'crushes' I had on females while growing up" 3. "I can't attribute the way I am to any one thing or any several things, I came from a good home and have a wonderful family that loves me."
J	Sees self feminine. Both roles in sexual relations	Father: cold, punitive, not-loving, bastard Mother: weak, warm, kind, loving	1. Poor family background 2. First sexual experience with female—"Great" 3. "My mother and poor relationships with father figures"
K	Feminine Bisexual	Father: weak, alcoholic Mother: dominant	1. Not well-adjusted 2. "Mature enough to make choice, satisfied with being bisexual, not narrow minded either way"

TABLE II
CONTRIBUTING CAUSAL FACTORS—(Continued)

Letter	Type of Sexual Role; Masculine, Feminine or (Both): Bisexual	Parents	Contributing Factors in Causation
L	Sees self feminine. Both roles in sexual relations	Father: weak Mother: dominant, "smothering" Parents divorced when *L* was four years old	1. Broken home 2. First sexual experience with female—"Glorious" (Never had sexual relations with male) 3. "I did not learn to love men. Father gone at age 4, my interests as a child were those of boys. I dislike the cramping role which our society sets for women."
M	Sees self feminine. Both roles in sexual relations	Father: weak Mother: dominant	1. Unstable home life 2. First experience sexually with female—"Very right" 3. "My mother had (unconsciously) needed me to be a lesbian, thus acting out her own unconscious homosexual feelings."
N	Masculine	Father: dominant, punitive, warm, not-loving Mother: dominant, kind, warm, loving	1. First sexual experience with female—"Fine" 2. "Either at conception or birth"
O	Feminine Bisexual	Step-father: molested her and tried to rape her when 4 months pregnant	1. Poor family background 2. Had baby out of wedlock 3. "Fear of pregnancy, met lesbian, she was like a wonderful aunt or mother"
P	Masculine	Father: dominant Mother: weak Family background "normal"	1. First sexual experience with female 2. "Parents wanted a boy. They encouraged male characteristics" 3. "My mother's lack of interest in me"

TABLE II
CONTRIBUTING CAUSAL FACTORS—(Continued)

Let-ter	Type of Sexual Role; Masculine, Feminine or (Both): Bisexual	Parents		Contributing Factors in Causation
Q	Sees self feminine. Both roles in sexual relations	Father:	gentle	1. First sexual experience with female. (Never had sexual relations with male)
		Mother:	dominant	2. "Identified totally with Victorian father, independent and rebellious. Would not submit like my mother. I like men very much as friends, I just don't like penises."
R	Feminine	Father:	weak	1. First sexual experience with female
		Mother:	dominant	2. Broken home, parents divorced
				3. "Lack of proper opportunity to get to know boys of my own age and going to all girls schools."
S	Masculine	Father:	kind, warm, loving	1. First sexual experience with female. (Never had sexual relations with male)
		Mother:	kind, warm, loving	2. "I don't really know. I was the 'tomboy' type kid. I enjoyed things boys did. Attracted to girls in high school. I couldn't conceive of being feminine."
T	Masculine	Father:	dominant	1. First sexual experience with female. (Never had sexual relations with male)
		Mother:	weak	2. "I was in love with a mother symbol, who showed me affection at age 12. I developed a male ego and wished desperately that I was a boy."

TABLE II
CONTRIBUTING CAUSAL FACTORS—(Continued)

Let-ter	Type of Sexual Role; Masculine, Feminine or (Both): Bisexual	Parents	Contributing Factors in Causation
U	Feminine	Father: dominant, kind, warm, loving Mother: dominant, kind, warm, loving	1. "Feelings I couldn't compete with my mother. Inferiority complex when young, fear of being rejected by boys."
V	Masculine	Stepfather: dominant, punitive, cold, not-loving Mother: dominant, cold, kind, loving	1. First sexual experience with female—"Pleasure-able" 2. "I agree with those psychologists that my disposition towards lesbianism was determined prior to age five."
W	Sees self feminine. Both roles in sexual relations	Father: absent Mother: dominant "Grandmother raised me"	1. Divorce—broken home 2. "Mother never too conscious of me. Dad never home. Was sent to boarding schools and camps. Grew up around women and always enjoyed them."
X	Masculine	Father: dominant Mother: weak and psychotic	1. First sexual experience with female. (Never had sexual relations with male) 2. "I created for myself an imaginary world in which I was the perfect male. I was quite positive that I was in fact a man who had been born in a woman's body."
Y	Sees self feminine. Both roles in sexual relations	Father: warm, kind, silent, withdrawn Mother: dominant, cold, punitive	1. First sexual experience with male—"Disappointed" 2. "Prefer women, more satisfying sexually. Easier to live with. Lesbianism is positive. I've tried both."

TABLE II
CONTRIBUTING CAUSAL FACTORS—(Continued)

| Z | Masculine | Father: dominant, kind, warm, loving
Mother: dominant, kind, warm, loving
Good family background | 1. "I really don't know. More interested in females for as long as can remember. I'm happy the way I am." |

TABLE III
SUMMARY OF CAUSAL FACTORS

Type	Total Number	Causation Pattern
FEMININE		
Feminine	4	Unstable family life (all 4)
Bisexual	A, B, K, O	Trauma (3), A, B, O
Feminine	5	Unstable home life (2), C, R
	C, F, I, R, U	Father: weak; Mother: dominant (2) C, R
See themselves	7	Unstable home (5), E, J, L, M, W
feminine.	E, J, L, M, Q,	Father: weak; Mother: dominant (6)
Both roles in	W, Y	E, L, M, Q, W, Y
sexual relations		First sexual experience with female— "Satisfying" (4), J, L, M, Q
Feminine	16	Unstable home life 11/16
(total)		Father: weak; Mother: dominant 8/16
MASCULINE		
Masculine	9	Father: dominant; Mother: weak (5),
	G, H, N, P, S,	G, P, T, V, X
	T, V, X, Z	First sexual experience with female— "Satisfying" (7), H, N, P, S, T, V, X
		Crushes on girls when young (3), H, X, Z
		'Tomboy'—felt like a boy, raised as a boy (4), P, S, T, X
Sees self masculine	1	Broken home
Both roles in	D	Attachment to mother
sexual relations		
Masculine	10	First sexual experience with female——
(Total)		"Satisfying" 7/10
		Father: dominant; Mother: weak 5/10
TOTAL	26	**No Universal Casual Pattern**

THE INDIVIDUAL CASES

A

A is a thirty-five-year-old secretary who is bisexual in her sexual relations. Her father's death when she was only eight years old was a traumatic experience, as she had liked her father best and describes him as dominant, warm, kind, and loving. Her mother is seen as weak, cold, punitive, and not-loving. She has a brother ten years older than she and a sister 15 years older, but she has never felt particularly close to either of them. After her father died, her brother became the head of the family, and *A* describes his behavior as being "very cruel and sadistic in his relationship with me. He would hurt and humiliate me." Her first sexual experience (intercourse) was with a man. This she describes as "very traumatic as the man was a pick-up. I felt used." Her father's death, her brother's cruel behavior, her unfulfilling sexual experience, and her mother's "rejection" evidently set the stage for her lifelong search for a woman who would be kind, warm, and loving to her. She sees women in general as being warm, but feels lesbianism is bad (morally), unhealthy (psychologically), and unsatisfying (physically). She thinks men in general are punitive and not loving. She seems to feel lost somewhere in the middle, not being able to have satisfying sexual relations with either sex. She considers that the factors that were influential in her becoming a lesbian were her brother (who "was cruel in his behavior towards me") and her mother (who "was too strict about my relationships with boys and would make me feel *guilty* if I was interested in boys"). If she could relive her life, she would definitely not become a lesbian because there is "too much unhappiness and loneliness."

A demonstrates a haphazard and abnormal profile on the Adjective Check List. The Defensiveness scale is highly abnormal (below 30), indicating that she was being hypocritical and deceiving in describing herself, that is, she was trying to "fake bad." *A* can be described as being overly anxious and apprehensive, extremely critical of herself and others, and given to frequent complaints about her circumstances.

B

B is a twenty-three-year-old babysitter who went to the eleventh grade in high school. She is now bisexual in her sexual relations. *B* suffered an extremely traumatic experience during her formative years; her stepfather raped her when she was eight years of age. All she says about this incident is that it "hurt." She sees her stepfather as dominant, cold, punitive, and not-loving. She does not respect him at all. She respects her mother because "she respects me." She pictures her mother as dominant, warm, punitive, and loving. She has two brothers, aged ten and one-and-a-half years, and four sisters, aged twenty-four, twenty-two, twenty-one, and seven years. She feels much closer to the twenty-two-year-old sister than to any of the others because they are closer in age and "thought alike." *B* feels that lesbianism is good (morally), healthy (psychologically), and satisfying (physically). *B* thinks the main factor contributing to her becoming a lesbian was "being raped at age eight and constantly being bothered by my stepfather." *B* states she is "satisfied" being a lesbian and does not want to change.

B projects an abnormal profile on the Adjective Check List, with a highly deviant Defensiveness scale. The only interpretation that can be given is that she was dissimulating. To summarize *B*'s profile, she is deceptive, extremely troubled, and unhappy in the sexual adjustment she has chosen (i.e. bisexuality), an unhappiness that may stem from her traumatic experience during childhood, which has never been truly effectively resolved.

C

C is a twenty-year-old lesbian who has never had sexual intercourse with a man. Her father, whom she describes as weak, cold, kind, not-loving, and "spineless," is an alcoholic. She said her father "does not respect himself," therefore, she has no respect for him. Her mother, whom she sees as dominant, cold, punitive, not loving, and very unreasonable, is a psychotic individual. *C* does not respect her mother, for "she demands respect, but does not deserve it." She says, "My parents were not very affectionate toward each other. Father sleeps in the car. Mother beats up father. Not extremely well adjusted!" She has one sister, aged twenty-four, but is not very close to her. The attitude that sex is immoral, emphasized by her parents, made sex with men seem wrong. Her first and only sexual experience was with a woman. "Rebellious and full of curiosity my sister's friend and I formed a deep friendship. I fell in love with her intellectually—*also I had never had a real friend before.* After four months of this deep friendship we entered into a lesbian relationship. She had been a *butch lesbian* for a number of years already. She seduced me." The seduction happened when *C* was sixteen. As she says, "The thing preventing me from changing (and becoming heterosexual) is the fact that I am in love. I realize that I could never hope to find another love so deep and beautiful as the one I have now which has lasted four years!" It is said that the only girl who can be seduced is the one who wants to be seduced. *C* obviously needed affection, she had never had a real friend before, and she decided to experiment.

C has only two high scores on the Adjective Check List, Total Number Checked and Succorance; and two low scores: Self-Confidence and Dominance. *C* can be described as emotional, wholesome, conservative, enthusiastic, adventurous, frank, and helpful. She is active, apparently means well, but tends to blunder. She needs and seeks the support of others; for example, she seems very dependent on her partner. *C* has a trusting personality and a naïve faith in the integrity and benevolence of others. She is unsure of herself and avoids interpersonal contacts, situations calling for choice and decision-making. In summary, *C* is a mild, wholesome, preoccupied, reserved, and unassuming individual. She has difficulty in mobilizing herself and taking action, preferring inaction and contemplation.

D

D is a woman forty-one years of age who would "rather not say" what her occupation is. She is a college graduate and a Unitarian by faith. She grew up in a broken home—her father, who is described as kind, warm, and loving, left because *D*'s mother could not satisfy him sexually. The mother, described as dominant, cold, punitive, and kind, loving and not-loving, and seductive, was very victorian about sex. "She had attitudes of shame, prudery, and guilt. If she were less conventional and freer she would probably have been 'gay'." *D* has one brother forty-three years old, to whom she felt very close in childhood. They are still friends. She considers herself to be very masculine. She has had sexual intercourse with men but the experiences were all "disappointing;" she has "avoided men during the past three years." She attributes her lesbianism to "My attachment to my mother. My resentment of my brother's favored place." *D*'s lesbianism appears to be symbolic of her desire for mother-love, enhanced by her jealousy of her brother and perhaps the rejection by her father. She says she wants to "overcome my inhibitions that block (my) realizing physical affairs where I am most attracted. Where there is the most meaning. I fear failure most. I also fear my life (being taken over) by someone skilled in manipulation of people."

D seems to be ambivalent and confused, as indicated by her Adjective Check List profile. *D*'s score on Defensiveness is so highly deviant that the profile as whole is invalid. She is extremely anxious, perplexed, fearful, and self-critical.

E

E is in the graphics trade and is twenty-two years of age. She comes from a home that was in many ways unstable. Her father is described as weak, warm, kind, loving, and her mother as dominant, cold, punitive, and not-loving. She states, "My parents were not affectionate to one another, and didn't even enjoy each other's company. Their sex life has always been very unsatisfactory to both of them. My mother doesn't like sex. My father has carried on various affairs throughout their marriage." She does not respect her father because he let himself and her family be pushed around by her mother for 20 years. She does not respect her mother either because she does not respect herself and she has led a miserably unhappy life, not one that *E* has any desire to imitate. Her older sister, aged twenty-seven (she also has a sister twenty-one years old) was a prostitute in her teens and became pregnant. When she was seventeen, *E*'s parents were overly strict with her because they feared she would follow in her sister's footsteps. When she was thirteen, *E* was sexually seduced by her brother-in-law. As she put it, "I was not at all ready for sex. I didn't respond at all. I realized the meaning of what happened later and was very disappointed in my older sister's husband." This was her only sexual intercourse with a man. She views all men as dominant, cold, punitive, and not-loving. In describing the experiences in her life that were influential in her becoming a lesbian she states, "I didn't outgrow an infantile desire for very close physical contact with mother. My own mother wasn't interested so I looked elsewhere, to my friends' mothers and women teachers. In my teens I had a few intense crushes on teachers, one from age twelve to fifteen and one from fifteen to seventeen. When I was fourteen, about five months after I realized my older sister was pregnant, I met a boy and 'went steady' with him for nine months. We were very much interested in each other—sex would have developed later. My parents were afraid of my interest in him so they put a sudden stop to our romance. I did not want to date any other boy. At the same time, my interest in girls my own age became quite physical and when I was sixteen, I asked two girls to neck with me (unaware of the word homosexual or the taboo). Both of the girls turned me down, but one referred me to a lesbian friend of her mother's. This older lesbian was my first lover, I am now in gay life and seeking a mate, believing that my offense against society is my existence, and not my behavior. I am a lesbian because I have learned to seek love from women, not men, probably from never having had a satisfactory heterosexual relationship around me (such as between one's parents), to show me that love from men is possible and uniquely satisfying."

E has high Adjective Check List scores in Favorable Adjectives Checked, Lability, Intraception, Exhibition, and Counseling Readiness, and low scores in only Deference. She seems motivated by a strong desire to do well and to impress others, but always by virtue of hard work. She is spontaneous, excitable, nervous, and impelled toward new experiences in an endless flight from her problems. She is intelligent, capable, and conscientious. However, this seems to go to her head, so that she is self-centered and even narcissistic. In sum, *E* is independent, energetic, ambitious, egotistical, but at the same time quick-tempered and irritable.

F

F is a forty-three-year-old electronics assembler, of the Baptist faith. She has two brothers aged twenty-six and forty, and one sister aged forty-one. Her father is pictured as dominant, kind, cold, and loving. She also calls him a "chaser," even though she feels her parents were affectionate and well-adjusted sexually. Her first sexual experience was with a woman. She describes it "as though it was the natural thing to do." In explaining the factors that led her to lesbianism she states, "I think that I was the oldest of four children (also being a girl) had every part of my becoming a lesbian." In reply to the question, "If you could relive your life, would you become a lesbian?" She put, "Yes. I would because as a lesbian I've been happier, healthier, more at ease, and had more material things, friends included, and have been closer to my family than before."

F had high scores on the Adjective Check List scales: Total Number Adjectives Checked, Favorable Adjectives Checked, Self-Control, Personal Adjustment, Achievement, Endurance, Order, Heterosexuality, and two low scores, Unfavorable Adjectives Checked, and Succorance. *F* appears to be motivated by a strong desire to perform hard work, impress others, and engage in conventional endeavors. Others would tend to see her lacking in nerve and quickness of mind. She is a diligent, practical, and loyal worker. At the same time there is an element of overcontrol, too much emphasis on the proper means for attaining the ends of social living. *F* is generally unduly optimistic in her dealings with others. Her Baptist upbringing is reflected in her overconcern with truth and the gospel. *F* received a high score in Heterosexuality, indicating just the opposite of her expressed feelings toward men. In summation, *F* is prudent, self-sufficient, sincere, and somewhat dependable but at the cost of her individuality and spontaneity.

G

G is a typesetter and typist. Her family was made up of a dominant, cold, kind, and loving father, a weak, cold, kind, and loving mother, four brothers, aged forty-three, forty-one, thirty-nine, and twenty-eight, one sister aged twenty-nine, and *G* aged thirty-four. Neither parent displayed any overt affection either toward each other or toward the children. *G* left home when she was eighteen years old. Her first sexual experience was with a

man. As she describes it, "I was disappointed and pregnant." She
has since given men up and she herself plays the masculine role
in her lesbian relations. G feels that lesbianism is bad (morally),
very unhealthy (psychologically), but very satisfying (physically).
She lists the following factors as influential in her becoming a
lesbian: "(1) I never wanted to be married and live like the
people I saw around me—I still don't. (2) Fear of pregnancy. (3)
I began to see women as my brothers saw them and it was fun and
pleasant. (4) With women I have a feeling of 'protectiveness', of
warmth. With men I have never felt anything." The only difference G noted between "mother" and "women in general" was the
difference between "cold" and "warm," respectively.

G had only three high scores on her Adjective Check List profile: Total Number Checked, Self-Confidence, and Autonomy. G
is active, adventurous, conservative, means well, but tends to
blunder. She is assertive, affiliative, outgoing, forceful, self-confident, determined, ambitious, and opportunistic. She generally is
concerned about making a good impression, and is not above cut-
ting a few corners to achieve this objective. G is independent,
autonomous, self-willed, quick in temperament and reaction, and
impulsive. She prefers complexity and variety, and dislikes de-
lay, caution, and deliberation.

H

H is a twenty-six-year-old photofinisher who is an only child.
The only distinction she notes between her father and mother is
that the father was kind and the mother punitive. Her parents
were not affectionate in front of her. H's first sexual experience
was with a woman and she relates, "It was wonderful!" She has
never had sexual intercourse with a man and does not desire it.
She sees herself as masculine. Although she saw her mother as
punitive, she sees women in general as kind; while she saw her
father as warm, kind, and loving, she sees men in general as cold,
punitive, and not-loving. She explains how she became a lesbian
in these words: "I always wanted an older sister and began mentally choosing them. I always worshipped the ones I chose. I went to
YWCA camp for 6 summers where I was in 7th heaven. I went
through more crushes than a 5 year old goes through sox. When I

was around 10 years old I was severely reprimanded for letting my male cousin (15) play with me."

H's high scores on the Adjective Check List are Order, Abasement, Deference, Counseling Readiness, while her low scores are Self-Confidence, Heterosexuality, Exhibition, and Change. *H* is usually sincere and dependable but at some cost to her individuality. Her main problem is self-acceptance. She sees herself as weak, undeserving, and as facing the world with anxiety. *H*'s behavior is often self-punishing and self-effacing. She is self-denying not so much out of any fear of others or inferiority to them as out of preference for anonymity and freedom from stress and external demands. She attends modestly to her affairs, seeking little, and yielding always to any reasonable claim by another. She is dispirited, inhibited, shrewd, and calculating in her interpersonal relationships. *H* is apathetic, self-doubting, and has undue inhibition of impulse. She has difficulty in mobilizing herself and taking action, preferring inaction and contemplation. In summary, *H* lacks verve and energy, is patient, obliging, and predominantly worries about herself.

I

I is a twenty-seven-year-old administration instructor. Her parents seem fairly well adjusted sexually, as she says "They've always shared a double bed." They were openly affectionate in the home. *I* has two brothers aged nineteen and twenty-one and one sister aged twenty-five. She sees her mother as dominant, warm, kind, and loving, while she sees women in general as weak, warm, kind, and loving. Her father is seen as warm, kind, and loving while men in general are seen as dominant, cold, kind, and loving. In trying to figure out why she became a lesbian, she decided: "I have often wondered as I cannot attribute the way I am to any one thing or any several things. I come from a good middle-class home, have a wonderful family that loves me, am the oldest of four children and perhaps a little more responsible while we were growing up. I feel that I am a well-adjusted person who is liked by people with whom I come in contact. I can remember having crushes on girls while growing up and more so than boys. I think

I am more of a dominating person than one to be dominated upon and would rather care for someone than be cared for. . . . The general public pictures lesbians as unhappy women looking like and wanting to become men. I am sure if I am as happy as I am that there must be many others like myself around."

I had eight high scores on the Adjective Check List including Total Number Checked, Favorable Adjectives Checked, Self-Confidence, Self-Control, Achievement, Endurance, Nurturance, and Affiliation. Her low scores were Unfavorable Adjectives Checked, and Succorance. *I* is of a helpful, nurturant disposition, but sometimes is too bland and self-disciplined. Her dependability and benevolence are worthy qualities, but she may nonetheless be too conventional and solicitous of another person. She is by nature conventional, but because of a sense of rectitude she finds herself championing unpopular causes. *I* is seen as intelligent and hard-working. She is determined to do well and usually succeeds. Her dealings with other people may be unduly trusting and overly optimistic. She is very concerned about creating a good impression and will say or do things against her grain to provide herself with a "good image." She claims to be well-adjusted and she probably is. However, she usually keeps this quiet and has a sort of quiet confidence in her own worth and capability.

J

J is a twenty-year-old PBX operator who was raised as a Catholic. She feels she became a lesbian because of her "mother and poor relationships with father figures." She describes her father as a bastard, weak, cold, punitive, and not-loving, her mother as weak, warm, kind, and loving. Her home life was rather unstable, her parents having divorced and each remarried. She has lived with both of her parents and their families and in a foster home. She filled out the questionnaire tersely. For example, in describing her first sexual experience she wrote, "Female—Great." In reply to the question concerned with becoming a lesbian again if you could relive your life she answered, "I wouldn't change any part of my life. I like (basically) the person I am."

J's Adjective Check List was filled out fully in marked contrast to the questionnaire. She has high scores in Total Number Checked, Favorable Adjectives Checked, Self-Confidence, Dominance, Heterosexuality, Autonomy, Aggression, Change, and Counseling Readiness, and only two low scores, Abasement and Deference. *J* is characterized by a brisk tempo, a confident manner, and effective behavior. She is independent, energetic, takes pleasure in change, likes to supervise and direct others, and to express her will. She has confidence in herself and welcomes challenges to be found in disorder and complexity. All is not on the positive side, however, for *J* worries about herself, she feels left out of things, and is unable to enjoy life to the full. She is aggressive and competitive, and seeks to win, to vanquish, and views others as rivals. Her impulses are strong, but often undercontrolled. *J*'s intellectual talents are excellent and she derives pleasure from their exercise. In sum, *J* is confident of her ability to do what she wants and is direct and forthright in her behavior. Nevertheless, she is ambivalent about her situation in life.

K

K is a divorced, bisexual mother of two children, a thirteen-year-old boy and an eleven-year-old girl. She works as a telephone order clerk and is forty-three years old. Her family situation was not well-adjusted. Her father, an alcoholic, died when she was twenty-one or twenty-two. She has little recollection of him—"I seem to have blocked him out." She does recall that he was weak. She describes her mother as dominant and cold, and she was frightened and intimidated by her. Toward her father she felt only hate because of his constant drunkenness. She has two brothers, one a year older and another two years younger. This woman became a homosexual two-and-one-half years ago, after being heterosexual all her previous life. She said her first sexual experience was with a man and disappointing. But she added, "That didn't stop me—and I've had some swingin' men in my life and I don't hate them—I enjoy men, but discovered women, too." In answering the question "How did you become a lesbian" she replied, "I am mature enough to make a choice—of whom I like to associate with. I've been eight years in psychotherapy and I'm not intimidated by society in many respects. When I met Ruth it seemed very natural to fall in love and be loved by her. It was one of the most satisfying relationships in an affectionate way. I'm satisfied with being bisexual—not narrow minded either way."

K has only two high scores on the Adjective Check List, Total Number Checked and Counseling Readiness. Her low scores are Achievement, Dominance, Endurance, Heterosexuality, and Change. *K* is seeking stability and continuity in her environment, and is very apprehensive of ill-defined and risk-involving situations. She is patient and obliging, concerned about others, but lacks action and zest. *K* thinks too much, thus, dampens her vitality. She tends to be dispirited and calculating in relating to others. *K*'s behavior is erratic and she is intolerant of prolonged effort or attention and is apt to change in an abrupt and quixotic fashion.

L

L is a teacher, aged forty-nine, an agnostic who comes from a broken home. Her parents separated when she was four years old, because they were incompatible. She never really knew her father. She lived with her mother and with her grandparents, off and on. She characterizes her father as weak, while her mother is seen as dominant, warm, kind, loving, anxious, overprotective, and worrisome. She disliked the "smothering" qualities of her mother's care for herself and her one sister, two years younger than she. She had her first sexual experience with a woman and described it with the word—"Glorious." She has never had sexual intercourse with a man and does not have any desire to. She states, "In the course of my life I have been fortunate enough to have met two women whom I cared about deeply. With these two I was involved sexually." In explaining how and why she became a lesbian she states, "1. I did not learn to love men, apparently for some reason connected with the unsatisfactory marital situation in my home in the first four years. 2. I disliked the cramping role which our society sets for women and rebelled against it from earliest childhood. My interests as a child were those of boys but I was not allowed to indulge these interests." In reply to the question "Do you want to change now" she answers, "No, of course not. I can no more imagine wishing to be heterosexual than the average heterosexual can imagine wishing to be homosexual. I might add that one of my two profoundly satisfying relationships was indescribably beautiful and meaningful, that it has given justification and significance to my entire lifetime, regardless of the fact that it has not been a permanent relationship."

L has five high Adjective Check List scores: Endurance, Order, Abasement, Deference, and Counseling Readiness. Her low scores were twelve: Total Number Checked, Defensiveness, Favorable Adjectives Checked, Self-Confidence, Lability, Achievement, Dominance, Nurturance, Affiliation, Heterosexuality, Exhibition, and Change. L checked only 51 adjectives out of 300, indicating a quiet, reserved, and cautious person. She is apt to think originally and inventively, but is less effective in getting things done. She tends to be anxious and self-critical and is often given to complaints about her circumstances. She has difficulty in mobilizing herself to take action, preferring inaction and contemplation. Others would see L as unassuming, forgetful, mild, preoccupied, and retiring. She is routinized, planful, and conventional. In sum, she is calculating, inhibited, sincere, dependable at the cost of losing some of her individuality and vitality.

M

M is a forty-three-year-old medical secretary. Her father is described as passive, weak, kind, warm, and loving, whereas her mother is seen as dominant, punitive, cold, and not-loving. M has two brothers aged forty-one and thirty-eight, and three sisters aged thirty-six, thirty-one, and twenty-six. M's first sexual experience was with a female and "It seemed very 'right' to me and what I had unknowingly been searching for for a long time." Although she admits, "From a strictly mechanical point of view certainly the male-female combination has its advantages. However, if one doesn't like it or fears it or any of a dozen things the mechanical disadvantages seem minor." As to why she became a lesbian, she says, "It became clear to me during the course of a rather prolonged analysis that my mother had (unconsciously) needed me to be a lesbian, and thus act out her own unconscious homosexual feelings."

M's replies were limited on both the questionnaire and the Adjective Check List. She checked only 53 adjectives out of 300. Her high scores are Unfavorable Adjectives Checked, Counseling Readiness, and her low scores Total Number Checked, Defensiveness, Achievement, Favorable Adjectives Checked, Nurturance, Affiliation, and Heterosexuality. *M* tends to be critical of herself, is anxious and apprehensive. To offset her anxiety she is seen to be pleasure-seeking, clever, and original in thought and behavior. *M* seems to be somewhat withdrawn and dissatisfied with her life at present. One of *M*'s main problems is that she is too self-centered and pays too little attention to the feelings and wishes of others. In general, she tends to be less trusting, more pessimistic about life, and restless in any situation that intensifies or prolongs her contacts with others.

N

N is a forty-four-year-old kennel owner who holds a law degree. Her father is a lawyer, also. She comes from a Catholic home and has two brothers aged forty and thirty-four. Her father is described as dominant, punitive, warm, and not-loving. Also, "he is a typical sexy male." *N*'s mother is described as dominant, warm, kind, and loving. Her parents were very puritan in their sexual attitudes. Her first sexual experience was with a woman and the one word that describes it was "Fine." She experienced sexual intercourse with a man only once. It was with an Army gynecologist, so that she could get his help in getting a military discharge. *N* sees herself as masculine and feels that she became a lesbian "either at birth or conception." This hereditary viewpoint takes the responsibility off her shoulders and places it on her parents.

N has four high Adjective Check List scores: Lability, Intraception, Aggression, and Counseling Readiness, and four low scores—Defensiveness, Endurance, Affiliation, and Deference. She seeks to win in life and views others as rivals. Her impulses are strong but coupled with a sense of reflection and seriousness. She is capable, conscientious, and knowledgeable. Her intellectual capacities are excellent and she derives pleasure from mental exercises. *N* tends to be spontaneous, excitable, temperamental, restless, nervous, and high-strung. In sum, she is individualistic, strong-willed, energetic, likes to supervise, and is self-critical in a constructive manner.

O

O is a twenty-year-old Jewish supervisor-foreman in a photo-finishing plant. She comes from a very poor family environment. Her mother was a weak person, a drunk and a flirt. "She didn't seem to mind the beatings given her by my stepfather." Her mother divorced her real father when *O* was only three. The stepfather frequently beat *O* as well as her mother. The stepfather also forceably sexually molested *O* on several occasions. As *O* put it, "No normal homelife. No laughter, no song, no self-respect." *O* ran away from home when she was sixteen and became pregnant a year later. She was sent home by the police. Her stepfather tried to rape her when she was four months pregnant. She describes how she thought she became a lesbian: "I had my baby and gave it up for adoption. I only had $2.50 to my name. Then I met Anne. I was really desperate for warmth and love. I didn't want men, I was afraid I'd get pregnant again. Mary Anne helped me so much like a wonderful aunt or mother, aside from the sex. My lover is twelve years older than me." She said if she could live her life over again she would have become a lesbian a lot sooner.

O's high Adjective Check List scores are Total Number Checked, Unfavorable Adjectives Checked, Heterosexuality, Exhibition, Aggression, Change, Succorance, Counseling Readiness. She has only two low scores—Defensiveness and Personal Adjustment. *O* tends to be extremely critical of herself, anxious, and apprehensive. She is emotional, wholesome, frank, and helpful. However, *O* sees herself at odds with other people and as moody and dissatisfied. Observers would see her as aloof, defensive, anxious, inhibited, withdrawn, and unfriendly. She is especially apprehensive about ill-defined situations. In sum, *O* is dependent upon others, seeks support, and expects to find it. She has many problems and is presently pessimistic about her ability to resolve them constructively.

P

P is a forty-seven-year-old Jewish registered nurse who has two sisters aged forty-eight and thirty-nine. She was closer to the older one in her childhood years. Her parents were middle-class and had a seemingly satisfying relationship with each other. She describes her father as dominant, warm, punitive, and loving. Her mother is pictured as weak, suspicious, and punitive. *P* sees herself as quite masculine, which is understandable after reading her explanation of the factors influential in her becoming a lesbian. "1. Primarily, the fact that my parents wanted a male child and seemed to encourage any male characteristics I displayed—I was told by everyone 'you're just like your father' and so was led to emulate him in every way (including his uncontrollable temper). 2. My mother's lack of trust. My dates were viewed with suspicion. Even after the age of eighteen." If given another opportunity to live her life over, *P* felt that she would not become a lesbian, because "heterosexual life is usually simpler because it is more accepted." However, in "this life" she does not want to change to heterosexual because, "I have as happy and as satisfying a life as most women I know who have married men."

P's high Adjective Check List scores are Affiliation and Counseling Readiness, and her low scores Abasement and Deference. *P* is energetic, spontaneous, optimistic, poised, independent, productive, and decisive. She likes attention, likes to direct others, her manner is confident, her behavior effective, and she expresses herself well. *P* is adaptable and anxious to please but tends to worry about herself and her present status. At times, she even feels left out of things and is unable to enjoy life to its fullest.

Q

Q is a forty-year-old medical clerk and typist who was trained as a registered nurse. She is now an atheist, and stated, "I attended church regularly up to age thirty-three. Then I came to Sinful, California." As a child she loved and respected her parents, whom she describes as warm, kind, and loving. She adds that her father is gentle but tends to worry a lot. She has two sisters, one thirty-nine, the other thirty. She was very close to the thirty-year-old sister in childhood and still is. Q had her first sexual experience with a woman at age nineteen, and "loved it—decided then and there that was for me. For maybe five years afterward I had pangs of guilt but I never deviated from my deviation." She has never had sexual intercourse with a man. She says, "I like men very much—I just don't like penises. To me they're silly and I couldn't be attracted to something silly. Or I never have been anyway." She considers lesbianism very good (morally), very healthy (psychologically), and very satisfying (physically). She describes how she thinks she became a lesbian in the following words: "I was the daughter of a Victorian father—but I was very much like him in independence and rebelliousness. I guess I chose very early not to become a partner in such a marriage, since I wasn't willing to give the man as much deference as my mother gave my father—or as I thought she did." She also stated, "I felt psychologically closer to my father because we were both individualistic and stubborn, etc." Q considers herself to be masculine and has been living with the same woman for 14 years. She describes this relationship as "most rewarding sexually, psychologically, and whatever other way you can think of."

Q has several high Adjective Check List scores: Favorable Adjectives Checked, Self-Confidence, Lability, Personal Adjustment, Dominance, Endurance, and Order; and three low scores: Succorance, Abasement, and Deference. In many ways she is like her described father, the following traits being characteristic of them both: independent, forceful, strong-willed, persevering, autonomous, energetic, and spontaneous. Also like her father, she likes attention, likes to supervise and direct others, and to express her will. She has sincere concern with behaving appropriately and with doing one's duty (like her mother). Her psychological equilibrium, the balance of forces, is an uneasy one and she seems impelled toward change and new experience in an endless flight from her perplexities. By nature she is conventional but she nonetheless (because of a sense of rectitude) finds herself championing unconventional ideas and unpopular causes. One noteworthy thing is that she is not deferent like her mother. *Q*, in sum, is optimistic, independent, self-sufficient, and productive. She has a sort of quiet confidence in her own worth and capability.

R

R is a telephone operator, twenty-four years of age. She is of the Catholic faith and comes from a divorced home. Her father is seen as weak, kind, cold, not-loving, quiet, and reserved. Her mother is described as dominant, punitive, warm, and loving. Her first sexual experience was with a woman. *R* describes it thus: "I was scared and confused but was satisfied and at the same time happy—I felt I was doing something wrong and yet I didn't know what or why." *R* stated her reasons briefly on why and how she became a lesbian: "Lack of proper opportunity to get to know boys of my own age and going to an all girl high school." She mentioned that if she had a choice to relive her life, "I would not want to be a woman at all. I would want to be a man. A man, to me, has much more freedom than a woman and more opportunity for adventuresome deeds. But if I had to be a woman I would be a lesbian. I'm happy and I wouldn't want it any other way."

Although *R* says over and over in her questionnaire "I'm happy being a lesbian," "I don't want to change," her Adjective Check List profile indicates a different feeling. Her high scores were in Unfavorable Adjectives Checked, Succorance, Abasement, Counseling Readiness, and her low—Total Number Checked, Defensiveness, Favorable Adjectives Checked, Personal Adjustment, Dominance, Nurturance, Affiliation, Heterosexuality, and Exhibition. Her extremely high scores in Succorance and Abasement mean that she is not only submissive and self-effacing, but that she also appears to have problems of self-acceptance. She sees herself as totally dependent on others, seeking support, weak, undeserving, and facing the world with much anxiety. She is self-punishing in much of her behavior, perhaps in the hope of forestalling criticism and rejection from without. *R* is rebellious, arrogant, careless, conceited, and cynical. She tends to be a disbeliever, a skeptic, and a threat to the complacent beliefs of her fellows. In total, R is unsure of herself, apathetic, and self-doubting.

S

S is a thirty-five-year-old clerk. As a child she felt closer to her father and liked him best. She saw him as kind, warm, and loving, as was her mother. Her family is a large one—four brothers aged fifty-one, forty-five, forty-three, and thirty-eight, and one sister aged forty-six. Her parents showed very little affection toward each other. However, the father "took time out with me." Her first sexual experience was with a woman. S stated, "I felt nervous about it afterwards but after a short while it became a regular thing." It became a lasting thing too—S has never had sexual intercourse with a man. She sees herself as a quite masculine person who is searching for a feminine partner who will be capable of love, understanding, and kindness. "I was the 'tomboy' type kid being raised with three of my brothers. Only one other girl in the neighborhood. I enjoyed the things boys did. Never liked girlish occupations and in my teens found myself attracted to females." This was S's explanation of how she became a lesbian. "Yes" was her answer to the question "Would you become a lesbian if you could relive your life." She added, "Even after a few unhappy relationships I enjoy my life. Being a lesbian comes so natural I'm not forced—I'm able to love my way. I couldn't conceive of being feminine."

S has six high Adjective Check List scores: Favorable Adjectives Checked, Self-Confidence, Achievement, Dominance, Exhibition, and Autonomy. Her low scores are Succorance and Abasement. S is independent, resourceful, and self-sufficient, but at the same time prudent and circumspect. She has a sort of reserved self-confidence in her own worth and abilities. Not fearing others, S is poised, self-assured, and able to meet situations with aplomb, but at the same time she is quick tempered and irritable. In her dealings with others she is apt to be opportunistic. She is intelligent and hard-working, forceful, strong-willed, and of a persevering nature. In sum, S is independent, and autonomous, but also assertive and self-willed.

T

T is a secretary-student, twenty-three years old. She has one brother aged twenty and a sister aged ten. Her family was headed by a dominant, kind, warm, not-loving, perfectionistic, and devoutly Catholic father. The mother was, in contrast, weak, warm, kind, and loving but unaffectionate. *T*'s first sexual experience was with a female. As she stated concerning this, "There was no guilt. I was in love with a 'mother symbol' who showed me affection. Age 12. By this time I think I had developed a male's ego and was desperately wishing I would have been a boy, so naturally I would have enjoyed sex with a woman." She has never had sexual intercourse with a male (and doesn't plan to). She considers herself to be very masculine. She looks for feminine characteristics, preferably blonde hair, and emphasizes a warm smile. *T* replied to the question "Why and how did you become a lesbian": "It seems all the emphasis as to causation is put on the parents. In my case, even though I lived with both parents, my grandmother, who visited us every day and did all the babysitting for us, influenced me and my wanting to be a male. She always favored boys and so she did my brother. Also, affection was never displayed in our family. I always knew they loved me, but I had to discover this myself rationally. I have never had problems like a lot of other lesbians whose fathers attacked them, lack of real mother-love, separated parents. . . ." Concerning lesbianism, *T* feels "the society is wrong; lesbianism is not immoral, nor is it unhealthy. . . . I could not live as a clinging vine; a housewife."

The only two Adjective Check List scores that are out of the normal range on *T*'s profile are Total Number Checked and Endurance (slightly high). *T* is typically self-controlled and responsible, but also idealistic and concerned about truth and justice. By nature she is conventional but may find herself (because of her concern) championing unpopular ideas or causes. *T* tends to be emotional, adventurous, wholesome, enthusiastic, frank, and helpful.

U

This forty-one-year-old administrative assistant is an individual who respects both of her parents as persons rather than just people. She described her parents exactly the same—dominant, kind, warm, and loving. She has one sister with whom she was very close in her childhood. Her mother was more affectionate than her father. *U*'s first sexual experience was with a male—"Sort of blah! I didn't feel badly about it— it seemed natural. I used to be bisexual. I have been living with a woman for a long time so I have not had sex with a man for many years." She explained the process of becoming a lesbian as it was to her: "Feeling I couldn't compete with my mother; inferiority complex when young (fear of being rejected by boys) ; in later years, the lack of sensitivity in males and their obsession with sex; finally, the girl I met! . . . I'm happy in this life and I'm too old to reorient myself to the submissive role of housewife."

U has three high Adjective Check List scores: Total Number Checked, Lability, Intraception, and two low scores—Succorance and Abasement. *U* is seen favorably as spontaneous, and unfavorably as nervous and excitable. She is emotional, helpful, conservative, and adventurous. Usually *U* is reflective and serious. She is also capable, conscientious, and intelligent. She is independent, resourceful, self-sufficient, optimistic, productive and decisive.

V

This forty-four-year-old bookkeeper and office manager is a metaphysicist by faith. She was closest to and liked her mother best during childhood. Her stepfather is described as dominant, punitive, cold, and not-loving. She never knew her real father. Her mother is seen as dominant, cold, kind, and loving. There was little or no affection expressed between *V*'s parents. *V* has one sister aged thirty-eight and she stated that she was never close to her. Her first sexual experience was with a girl. "It was very pleasurable. But instinctively I knew this was something I should not let anyone know about." *V* sees herself as masculine and is "searching for a girl with feminine appearance, softness of the skin, and shapely legs." In a long-term companion she looks for "love, warmth, tenderness, mutual respect, and understanding." Factors that led to her becoming a lesbian are: "As a child I played 'house' with the girls, and I always played the role of husband and father. I remember having a cowboy outfit which I was very proud of. . . . It seems to me that to get any place in life you had to be a boy. For a time I dreamed of some miraculous change. In adolescence I was attracted to girls. However, I agree with those psychologists that my disposition towards lesbianism was determined prior to age five." *V* has been living with the same partner for 14 years and she is quite happy with her life. "There is a warm companionship, a community of interests—we have good jobs, own our own home, etc."

V has high Adjective Check List scores in Self-Confidence, Achievement, Dominance, Autonomy, Change, and Counseling Readiness, and low scores in Abasement and Deference. *V* is energetic, vigorous, spontaneous, and independent. She likes attention, likes to dominate others, and to directly express her will. She feels that her life is not being lived to its fullest. Also, she is unduly anxious and worried about herself. Her tempo is brisk and her personality alert, intelligent, and diligent. *V* is an actionist, assertive, affiliative, outgoing, and strong-willed.

W

W is a secretary-general office worker, twenty-eight years old. Her parents were divorced when she was three and she did not know her father until she was twenty-four. Her grandmother raised her and she saw her mother only at night and on the weekends. She has one sister aged ten, who is from her mother's second marriage. *W*'s first sexual experience was with a male. As she stated, "I didn't enjoy it very much. There was no satisfaction physically or emotionally." She is feminine and is looking for a long-term companion who is "understanding, loving, mature, and has the ability to accept being loved in the same way." In describing how and why she became a lesbian, *W* writes: "I came from a broken home, was sent to boarding schools and summer camps. Grew up around women, and have always enjoyed them. . . . Also, I never liked the supervisor attitude of men . . . never had a stable homelife. Mother was never too conscious of me, Dad never home. I was very independent at 12 by necessity." Her reply to the question on change from the lesbian life: "No—

I enjoy my homosexuality, my sex life, my feeling of 'being at home' as a lesbian. I like it, that's all."

W's high Adjective Check List scores are in the Unfavorable Adjectives Checked, Succorance, and Counseling Readiness scales and low on Defensiveness, Favorable Adjectives Checked, Self-Confidence, Personal Adjustment, Dominance, Intraception, Nurturance, and Affiliation scales. *W* is very dependent on others (almost in an infantile manner), seeks support, and expects to find it. She feels worried about herself and tends to feel "left out." She is very skeptical, clever, and acute, but too self-centered and too little attentive to the feelings and wishes of others. She is somewhat aggressive in manner, and quickly becomes bored or impatient with any situation wherein direct action is not possible. She is a doer, not a thinker.

X

X, thirty years of age, received an annullment from her recent marriage because it was not consummated. She has never had sexual relations with a male. *X* works as a dictaphone and tape recorder transcriptionist and is a devout Roman Catholic who attends church, often daily. She commented that the priests seem to be more enlightened now. She thinks they are receiving psychological training since at confession they tell her not to worry. Homosexuality, they say, is only an emotional-personality problem—"Don't have misgivings about yourself"—and they are glad she has come to church. Both her parents are now deceased. She has one homosexual brother, aged thirty-five and a sister aged forty-eight. *X* described her father as dominant, punitive, cold, not-loving, and extremely patient. "Patient," she said, "since his wife was completely frigid and he never committed adultery to my knowledge." Her mother was seen as weak, kind, cold, not loving, mentally disturbed, over-scrupulous spiritually, and extremely "anal compulsive." She stated, "I respected my father because he worked six days a week for 45 years as a barber without ever missing a day or taking a vacation (this is hard to believe, but true)." She, however, "lacked respect for him because of his vulgarity." She stated, "I respected my mother because she was always home, raised us as good children, never drank or ran around or left us alone, etc. However, I lacked respect for her because of her going into hysterics just to gain pity." Her mother had started having hysterical "seizures" following the birth of her brother. She described her mother's seizures: "Suddenly she would become violently ill in a split second—after that she remembered nothing—but what happened was she would roll her eyes upwards and flail her limbs violently, often falling to the floor and shout, "Oh my Jesus Mercy, Oh my Jesus Mercy." Her mother blamed her seizures on the brother for she never had them until after he was born. X stated, "She even attempted killing him on several occasions during her hysterical tantrums. Once I recall it took both my father and I to keep her from hitting him with a hatchet." She felt that her father had a suspicious nature and thought this to be "the direct result of his almost literally having to rape my mother, rather than ever having a warm and affectionate and truly satisfying relationship with her." X's home life was chaotic at best.

In answering the question concerning whether lesbianism is morally good or bad, psychologically healthy or unhealthy, physically satisfying or unsatisfying, X gives a well thought-out reply: "It seems this question is a loaded one. I say this because I feel that one cannot possibly give a definite answer to it. Mine is as follows: lesbianism is morally good or bad: I firmly believe that the act of sexual intercourse with one who is of one's own sex, when practiced *exclusively*—that is, when one never has had, has or intends to have normal intercourse with the opposite sex—is morally wrong. However, this sex act does *not* constitute lesbianism. Lesbianism is a personality problem. Its dominant characteristic is the fact that one is unable to perform the sex act with the opposite sex (or in other cases simply prefers the sex act with one's own sex) . However, much more is present here than a mere difference in sexual choice. As I expressed to an orthodox priest on one occasion: the fact that I choose a woman as my sexual object is the end result of my entire personality. In other words, my personality developed in a certain way so that it would, *of necessity, because of its very nature,* choose a woman rather than a man as its object of love, and therefore of sexual union. I did *not* first choose a woman as a sexual object, and therefore become labelled homosexual. First I chose to be of that bent of personality which is homosexual, and then I naturally chose a woman as my love object, or sex object. . . . Therefore, lesbianism as of, and by, itself is not morally bad. However, as I stated previously, I truly feel that the exclusive sex act with one's own sex is morally bad, but not because society as a whole frowns upon it, but rather because it does not fulfill the purpose of sexual gratification—which definitely is in the plan of God (no matter what our modernists try to say) to join together a man and a woman and thereby in the end to propagate the human race.

"Lesbianism is psychologically healthy or unhealthy. . . . If one knows what (lesbianism) really is, accepts all of its ramifications, comes to know oneself, and approaches life properly, there is no reason why it should be unhealthy. However, I feel it definitely can be when one does not know oneself and homosexuality well enough, because of the pressures of society upon this subject, as well as the moral guilt which one—either consciously or unconsciously—assumes when one is a *practicing* lesbian.

"Lesbianism is physically satisfying or unsatisfying. Naturally it is satisfying. One presumes here, of course, that one is speaking of a lesbian being the one who is practicing lesbianism. It is satisfying. And I might add, very satisfying."

X discusses the factors that contributed to her becoming a lesbian: "I associated strength and beauty with masculinity. I created for myself an imaginary world in which I was the perfect male, handsome, strong, . . . the whole bit. . . . This world came into being during my high school years . . . the reason lay in my parents' unhealthy attitudes and my experiences when growing up with my brother . . . society responded to the male more readily than to the female."

X states her views on the prognosis for homosexuality: "True homosexuality is incurable, because it is definitely the entire personality rather than a simple sexual choice, or a simple traumatic occurance or childhood or a fear of (the opposite sex)."

X has several high Adjective Check List scores: Total Number

Checked, Self-Control, Order, Intraception, Abasement, and Counseling Readiness; and three low scores: Dominance, Exhibition, and Aggression. X's intellectual talents are excellent and she derives pleasure from their exercise. She is a serious individual interested in and responsive to her obligations. She is sincere and dependable at the cost of her spontaneity and individuality to a certain degree. She has some problems of self-acceptance and faces the world with anxiety and foreboding. Her behavior is often self-punishing, perhaps in the hope of forestalling criticism and rejection from without. She is a conformist (as evidenced by her oftentimes daily church attendance) but is not necessarily lacking in courage or tenacity. In sum, X is reflective, serious, capable, conscientious, and knowledgeable. However, at times she is unsure of herself, indifferent to both the demands and the challenges of interpersonal life, and avoids situations calling for choice and decision-making.

Y

Y is a forty-two-year-old secretary. She is an only child and her parents both died recently. She described her father as warm, kind, silent, and withdrawn, while her mother was pictured as cold and punitive and "a beautiful woman who was rather self-centered." Her parents were two strong individuals who argued a lot with each other but loved each other a great deal. Y respected her parents. Her father was a person who told the truth and stood on his own two feet. Her mother was intelligent, sensitive, self-sufficient, a "grand old gal." Y's first sexual experience was with a male and she remarked about it—"Disappointed—that such a fuss could be made over such a nothing thing." About herself and lesbianism, she had this to say: "More satisfying sexually, easier to live with, have always preferred the company of men socially but prefer a woman as a companion (have tried both)." Her questionnaire was terse and the Adjective Check List gives us less insight into how Y sees herself.

Y's Adjective Check List profile is invalid due to the highly deviant score attained on the Defensiveness scale. She appears to be quite an anxious and apprehensive individual who is extremely critical of herself and others.

Z

Z is an electronics engineer, thirty-eight years old. Her home life was relatively stable. During her childhood she felt closer to her father and liked him the best. She describes both parents as affectionate, kind, warm, and loving. She has one younger brother, aged thirty-seven. Z's first sexual experience was with a male and she summed it up with "Indifferent." She sees herself as masculine. During the past four years she has lived with the same woman who is understanding, neat, and honest. Z does not really know what factors led to her becoming a lesbian. "For as long as I can remember I was more interested in girls. I tried to develop more than a friendly interest in boys but I never succeeded." In reply to the question concerning a change in sexuality, she stated, "No. As far as I'm concerned I am well-adjusted, have a good job and am as happy as anyone can be in this day and age."

She was right, for she is one of the best adjusted out of the twenty-six women, as indicated by her Adjective Check List profile. Her profile shows one high score—Favorable Adjectives Checked, and three low scores—Heterosexuality, Abasement, and Unfavorable Adjectives Checked. Z is motivated by a strong desire to do well and to impress others, but always by the virtue of hard work and conventional endeavor. The reaction of others is to see her as dependable, steady, conscientious, mannerly, and serious. She is tactful, slightly inhibited in her interpersonal relationships, but is optimistic about life around her. In summation, Z is poised, productive, decisive and, not fearing others, she is alert and responsive to them. Her tempo is brisk, her manner confident, and her behavior effective.

PART III

FEMALE HOMOSEXUALITY AS A WAY OF LIFE

"THE WORD HOMOSEXUALITY IS, OF COURSE, SHEERLY DESCRIPTIVE. IN MATTERS OF TASTE THERE SHOULD BE NO DISPUTE, BUT THERE IS A GREAT DEAL OF DISPUTE AS TO WHAT THIS CURIOUS PREFERENCE MEANS. NOT HOW REALLY EXCEPTIONAL OR HOW WIDELY PREVALENT IT IS, OR WHETHER IT IS IN AN ADVANCE STAGE OF DEVELOPMENT OR A RETARDED ONE, OR WHETHER IT REPRESENTS A PECULIARITY OF GENES OR A MISTAKEN KIND OF BRINGING UP.

"ONCE UPON A TIME WE THOUGHT WE KNEW ALL ABOUT IT. IT WAS A SIN, A CRIME, A DISEASE, AND/OR AN ANOMALY. WELL, SUDDENLY NOBODY SEEMS TO KNOW ANYTHING ABOUT IT. IT CEASES TO BE QUITE SO TABOO, AND YET NOT QUITE KOSHER. INDIVIDUALS MAY NOW CONFESS TO IT WITHOUT BEING THROWN OUT OF THE ROOM OR OUT OF COLLEGE. THERE ARE CLUBS AND FRONTS AND POLITICAL ORGANIZATIONS MADE UP OF PROFESSED HOMOSEXUAL INDIVIDUALS.

"THE HOMOSEXUAL (FREQUENTLY) DOES NOT CONSIDER HIMSELF [OR HERSELF] A FREAK OR A CRIPPLE OR AN ANOMALY OR A SICK MAN [OR WOMAN]. HE [OR SHE] CONSIDERS HIMSELF [OR HERSELF] ONE OF [EIGHT] MILLION OR MORE AMERICANS WITH THIS DIFFERENT PERSONAL PREFERENCE VALUE SYSTEM. MOST PSYCHIATRISTS REGARD IT AS A DISEASE OR AN ANOMALY. THERE IS A GREAT DEAL OF DIFFERENCE BETWEEN THESE TWO PROPOSITIONS BUT THERE IS NO DIFFERENCE IN THE MINDS AND FEELINGS OF MANY — IF NOT MOST — HOMOSEXUAL INDIVIDUALS. THEY DON'T WANT TO BE CONSIDERED EITHER ONE.

"ALL THIS SHOULD BE BORNE IN MIND WHEN WE NOTICE — AS ALL DO — THAT IN THE THEATER AND IN NUMEROUS NOVELS BITTER REPRISALS AND REPROACHES ARE DIRECTED BY THE AUTHORS AND PLAYWRIGHTS AGAINST THE HETEROSEXUAL ESTABLISHMENT. THE AUDIENCE GETS IT FULL IN THE FACE AND USUALLY DOESN'T KNOW WHAT HIT THEM OR WHY. AFTER THE

63

SHOW, AT THE CAST PARTY, THERE IS OFTEN GREAT HILARITY OVER THE UNPLEASANT SHOCK EFFECT THEY HAD BEEN ABLE TO INFLICT. SOME OF THE CRITICS KNOW AND BRAVELY RETALIATE; OTHERS ARE IN ON THE GAME" (MENNINGER, 1973) .

CHAPTER IV

IS LESBIANISM A HEALTHY LIFE STYLE OR AN ILLNESS?

"WE HAVE BEGUN to question whether homosexuality is really a psychologic illness or merely a way of life for much of our population" (Auerback, 1968, p. 170).

The only difference between the lesbian and other women is the choice of love object. Simon and Gagnon (1967) have shown that "in most cases the female homosexual follows conventional female patterns." Lesbianism is a way of life, not a sickness. The reason it has been considered an illness for over 50 years is that the few studies that have been done were drawn from captive samples of female homosexuals in prison or in psychotherapy. The lesbian has been a misfit in American culture, and leading a dual life has led to increased anxiety and emotional tension.

The majority of female homosexuals are mentally healthy and do not desire to be heterosexual. Female homosexuals have the same or a lower incidence of psychiatric disturbances when compared with matched heterosexual controls. No significant difference in the prevalence of neurotic disorders exists between female homosexuals and heterosexuals. These findings have been well documented by the numerous nonpatient studies outlined in Chapter 1. In a recent study by Asimos and Rosen (unpublished manuscript) it was found that lesbians do not have a higher incidence of depression, attempted suicide, or suicide such as was reported previously by Saghir and Robins (1971), Swanson *et al.* (1972), and as noted by Lyon and Martin (1972, p. 30). The results of the Adjective Check List tests in the study of lesbians reported in Chapter 2 revealed an overall normal pattern. Thompson *et al.* (1971) also utilized the Adjective Check List and found that the only difference between female homosexuals and their respective controls was that the lesbian group was "more self-confident."

It is time that we take note of Armon's pioneering work (1960) and adopt her position that lesbianism is not a clinical entity. Homosexuality as a mental disturbance should be deleted from the official diagnostic nomenclature of the American Psychiatric Association, where it is listed under "Section V. Personality disorders and certain other nonpsychotic mental disorders, Code 302.0 under sexual deviations." For too long we have generalized from a minority of lesbian psychiatric patients and applied a label of mental illness to the whole population of female homosexuals, an illogical and unjust process.

Kinsey *et al.* (1953) in one of the first objective investigations of human sexual behavior found among a *normal* population a group of healthy and well adjusted female homosexuals. Kinsey maintained that our life experiences teach us that our sexuality may be hetero-, homo- or bisexuality. He stated: "It is not so difficult to explain why a human animal does a particular thing sexually. It is more difficult to explain why each and every individual is not involved in every type of sexual activity" (p. 451). Freud (1951) did not consider homosexuality to be an illness. In "Letter to an American Mother" Freud wrote: "Homosexuality is assuredly no advantage . . . no degradation, it cannot be classified as an illness; we consider it to be a variation of the sexual function produced by a certain arrest of sexual development. Many highly respectable individuals of ancient and modern times have been homosexuals, several of the greatest men among them (Plato, Michelangelo, Leonardo da Vinci, etc.) It is a great injustice to persecute homosexuality as a crime and cruel too" (p. 787).

Szasz (1965), too, emphasized that lesbianism is a form of natural sexual behavior. He stated: "To argue that homosexuality is abnormal and heterosexuality normal is to cast various types of sexual conduct into the framework of health and disease" (p. 132). Cory (1964) stressed that lesbianism is a "learned condition" and emphasized that "therapy is the road for a few, but not for many" (p. 239) and that the great hope was to change society. To quote from a discussion between Wortis (1954) and Freud, "The question, though, is whether one ought to undertake to *cure* homosexuals as if they were diseased, or make their lot easier by making society more tolerant." "Naturally," said Freud, "The emphasis ought to be put on social measures; the only homosexuals one can attempt to cure are those who want to be changed" (p. 56).

CHAPTER V

CULTURAL FACTORS —
SOCIAL ATTITUDES AND VALUES

66 **A** LL THE EVIDENCE from comparative zoology . . . indicates
. . . that bisexuality or *ambisexuality* is the biologic norm
and that exclusive heterosexuality is a culturally imposed restric-
tion" (Marmor, 1965, p. 11). Our culture encourages heterosexuality, and marriage is prized above all. Homosexuality sym-
bolically threatens this cultural value as it used to threaten the
continuation of our species, although this should be no problem
with our present hope of curtailing overpopulation. Szasz (1965)
suggested: "We might even advocate homosexuality over heterosexuality; this choice could be supported as a contraceptive tech-
nique, especially for women intellectually or artistically gifted,
for whom the value of traditional feminine heterosexuality is a
barrier to achievement" (p. 137). Szasz stated further: "In our
day, homosexuality is a moral, political and social problem" (p.
138). The lack of religious involvement among lesbians is striking. As reported in Chapter 2, nearly half of the sample (12 out
of 26) had no religion. Of the remaining 14 women only three
attended church regularly. Probably these figures reflect the
church's lack of concern with the problem of homosexuality. The
government and police harass the lesbian; the courts take away
her children. Religious groups label her a sinner. Psychiatry calls
her mentally ill. How are we to change our own attitudes, our
professional opinions, and our society's values with regard to
lesbianism? One way is by education programs in our high schools,
colleges, and medical schools. Our religious leaders are going to
have to rethink their positions, as did the enlightened Catholic
priest mentioned in relation to individual case X in Chapter 3.
We will have to work for change within the psychiatric profession
to put homosexuality into proper perspective as a form of sexual
behavior, not as a mental illness. Political action such as newly

passed legislation in Illinois and several other states and in San Francisco[4] will set precedents for nationwide trends.

As women in general become liberated, so do they within the lesbian population. As a result, the strict *Butch-Femme* (masculine-feminine) role differentiation is less common and there is a trend for a more egalitarian type of relationship between female homosexuals. In addition, the relationship between female and male homosexual groups is changing. In contrast to previous times neither group is locked into rigidly defined roles and they are now beginning to interrelate and to join together in the pursuit of common goals.

---

4. Laws to permit sexual relations including homosexuality between consenting adults in private were passed in Illinois (1961) and in Connecticut, Oregon, Colorado, Ohio, North Dakota, Delaware, and Hawaii (1970's), and in April, 1972, San Francisco passed the first American civil rights legislation for homosexuals. The Board of Supervisors voted 10 to 1 for a prohibition against discrimination in employment on the basis of "sex or sexual orientation" by contractors doing business with the City and County of San Francisco.

CHAPTER VI

WHAT IS THE ETIOLOGY OF FEMALE HOMOSEXUALITY?

IT HAS BEEN SHOWN from the studies cited in Part I and from the etiological statements noted in the study reported in Part II that there are multiple causal factors for female homosexuality. Marmor (1965) summarized the critical points about etiology: "There is as yet no single constellation of factors that can adequately explain all homosexual deviations. The simple fact is that dominating and seductive mothers; weak, hostile, or detached fathers; and the multiple variations on these themes that are so often suggested as being etiologically significant in homosexuality abound in the histories of countless heterosexual individuals also and cannot therefore be *in themselves* specific causative factors. . . We are probably dealing with a condition that is not only multiply determined by psychodynamic, sociocultural, biological, and situational factors but also reflects the significance of subtle temporal, qualitative, and quantitative variables" (p. 5).

Lyon and Martin (1972) expressed similar ideas in different words: "Though many lesbians believe they were born that way, we tend to feel that persons are born sexual; not heterosexual or homosexual, just sexual. And the direction a girl's sexuality may take depends upon her individual circumstances and life experiences, and how she reacts to them" (p. 26). Kinsey's (1953) views on the etiology of female homosexuality are very similar.

From the study reported in this volume, and from those of Henry (1948), Kinsey (1953), and one reported by the British Medical Association (1955), one factor stands out as having more etiological weight than the others. This is the importance of the first sexual experience and whether it is pleasurable and positive with a woman or discomforting and negative with a man.

Armon's (1960) finding that homosexual women have a hostile-fearful conception of the feminine role may be one of the most important psychodynamic theories. This supports the etiological theory that lesbianism is a defense against hostility, fear, and guilt in relation to early significant but rejecting maternal objects. In my own study this seems to be an important etiological consideration in more than half of the cases (A,C,D,E,G,H,J,L, M,O,P,T,W,X and Y).

——————— CHAPTER VII ———————

IS THERE A PLACE FOR PSYCHIATRIC
TREATMENT OF LESBIANS?

IF A WOMAN feels driven to lesbianism, and the volitional choice
of a sexual object seems to be out of her control, then she might
qualify for psychiatric treatment. This would be like any sexual
behavior pattern that a person felt uncontrollably driven to carry
out but desired to change. The key point would be that the individual was uncomfortable and unhappy with being a lesbian
and wanted to change completely. The figures given for voluntary
patients being "cured" vary: Kaye *et al.* (1967) reported a 50 per
cent "cure" rate. Auerback's (1968) statement is probably more
realistic, "In most cases psychiatric treatment is unsuccessful" (p.
171).

Probably a more promising area would be in assisting women
who freely choose lesbianism to adjust and adapt to their sexuality.
This psychotherapy would be of a more supportive type. If a
self-identified lesbian is anxious, depressed, upset, or unhappy,
the important question is "why?" Pressures from society (peers,
family, church, employers, government, and doctors) do create
problems, produce stresses, and stimulate emotional disturbances
in lesbians (see the answers to question Number 32 in Chapter 2).
The psychiatric profession needs to help change the attitudes of
society through public and medical educational campaigns. However, since changing societal attitudes is a slow and arduous process, we need to begin now to help female homosexuals with their
problems. Adequate counseling and supportive psychotherapy for
individual mental disturbances and for communication problems
within the lesbian relationship should be readily available. A
model for this exists in San Francisco at the Center for Special
Problems, which treats a large number of homosexual clients in
individual, conjoint, and homogenous group therapy modalities.

Szasz (1965) correctly warned us against the compulsory or

72

involuntary treatment of female homosexuals as mentally ill patients in closed systems like government service, the military, and prisons.

I conclude this brief chapter on treatment with an important and pertinent statement from a recent report of a research study, comparing female homosexual and heterosexual psychiatric patients, by Swanson *et al.* (1972) : "The lesbian who seeks psychiatric treatment is similar to any other seriously troubled female patient. She is stressed, conflicted, and unsatisfied because of various conditions in her life, and her homosexuality is only one factor. Both because of reasons internal to the lesbian and because of society's pressures, the lesbian often experiences psychologic distress, but the clinical findings are not specific. This lack of significant historic and clinical factors specific to the lesbian makes a psychologic etiology of female homosexuality open to even more question than already exists" (p. 124) .

CHAPTER VIII

THE FUTURE AND THE NEED FOR FURTHER RESEARCH

THERE IS A need for large scale objective, nonbiased epidemiological studies of homosexual populations similar to the studies of heterosexuals done by Kinsey *et al.* (1953). This is necessary to confirm further the working hypothesis of this monograph, that lesbianism is a way of life and not a psychiatric illness. This should dispel permanently the present belief of many people, including psychiatrists, that female homosexuals are by definition seriously maladjusted. The classification of lesbianism as a mental disorder should be deleted from the Diagnostic Manual of the American Psychiatric Association.

A recent newspaper account (entitled "Lesbians Win Child Custody") illustrates another problem area: "Two mothers, both self-avowed lesbians and fundamentalist Christians, were awarded custody of their children (one had two and the other had four) by a Seattle Superior Court Judge on the condition that the two women live separately" (*This World,* 1973, p. 6). The court's condition that the two women live separately emphasizes that this was a pyrrhic victory. One purpose of this monograph is to provide information that might help change the individual's, the professionals', and society's view of the lesbian. Through sexual education and the political process the laws can be changed to stop discrimination against homosexuals.

There is a need for research studies in the area of lesbian mothers. Does the mother's homosexuality adversely influence the growing child's sexual identity? For the most part, the courts now take children away from lesbian mothers, perhaps causing more problems than they are solving. We therefore need follow-up studies of the natural and adopted children of lesbians.

The British Medical Association stated as early as 1955, "There is no evidence that homosexuality influences or is influenced by the reproductive complexus. If homosexuals marry and have children they do not appear to undergo any special disturbances either during pregnancy, childbirth or the puerperium" (p. 18).

There is a need to help society to adapt, adjust, and accept female homosexuals for what they are. There is a growing demand for supportive psychotherapy with an emphasis on helping female homosexuals adapt, adjust, and accept themselves for what they are. "True freedom . . . comes for the lesbian who sees herself for what she is—a woman. She accepts herself as a woman, loves being a woman, but unlike the heterosexual, she also desires being with a woman" (Cory, 1964, p. 83).

There is also a need for sexual therapy with homosexuals. Masters and Johnson are presently doing studies in this area. Masters has said, "More and more homosexual couples are feeling secure enough to come to us for help." He noted that these sexual problems correspond to those of heterosexual couples—the male with premature ejaculation and the lesbian who failed to experience orgasm. Masters and Johnson stated, "We tend to regard homosexuality as a natural function" (*Hospital Tribune*, 1972, p. 20).

APPENDIX I

QUESTIONNAIRE

QUESTIONNAIRE

Please answer all questions as completely as possible. If you need additional space or wish to make any extra comments pertaining to this questionnaire, the research, or other suggestions, feel free to do so on the attached blank sheets.

1. Occupation_____

2. Single_____ Married_____ Divorced or separated_____
   Do you have any children?_____
   Would you like to have any children?_____
   Do you think you will have any children?_____

3. Age_____

4. Educational background: High School_____
   Graduated_____ College_____ Degree_____
   Other (specify) _____

5. Religion _____ Do you attend church regularly? _____

6. Father's vocation _____
   Mother's vocation _____

7. In your childhood were you closer to your father _____
   or mother? _____

8. If you had to pick one parent as the one that you liked best which would you pick? Father_____ Mother_____

9. How would you describe your father? Underline one of the two in each pair of traits listed below and then add any others).
   a) Dominant or weak   c) Punitive or kind
   b) Warm or cold   d) Loving or not loving
   other _____

10. How would you describe your mother? (Follow same directions as above.)
    a) Dominant or weak   c) Punitive or kind
    b) Warm or cold   b) Loving or not loving
    other _____

11. Describe your parents' attitudes towards sex. (Were they affectionate towards each other? Well adjusted?) Explain this as fully as possible.

12. Were your parents open about sex? Did you discuss sex in your home?

13. Were your parents concerned about your sexual behavior outside of the home?

14. With whom did you grow up? Both parents_____
Mother_____ Father_____ Other (specify)
_____

15. To the best of your knowledge do your parents know you are a lesbian?
Yes_____ No_____ Don't know_____

16. Do you respect your father? Yes_____ No_____ Why or why not?

17. Do you respect your mother? Yes_____ No_____ Why or why not?

18. Do you have any brothers? How many? Their ages?

19. Do you have any sisters? How many? Their ages?

20. With whom were you the closest? Brothers_____
Sisters_____ (check one) Anyone in particular? Explain.

21. Are you now bisexual (having relations sexually with both males and females?)

22. Was your first sexual experience with a male or female? How did you feel about it?

23. Have you ever had sexual intercourse with a male? Yes_____
No_____

24. Rate yourself on these masculine-feminine scales: (circle appropriate number) How do you see yourself?
Masculine 1 2 3 4 / 5 6 7 8 Feminine
                          neutral
How do you think others see you?
Masculine 1 2 3 4 / 5 6 7 8 Feminine
                          neutral

25. Which role do you play in your sexual relations?
Masculine_____ Feminine_____ Both_____

26. Rate yourself on these scales describing how you feel about lesbianism: (circle appropriate number)
Morally   Good 1 2 3 4 5 6 7 8 Bad
Psychologically Healthy 1 2 3 4 5 6 7 8 Unhealthy
Physically Satisfying 1 2 3 4 5 6 7 8 Unsatisfying

27. a) How do you meet other lesbians? (For example, do you usually initiate the conversation? Where does it take place?)
   b) What cues do you use in deciding whether or not to ap-approach a woman?
   c) What physical characteristics are important to you in a woman sexual partner?
   d) What characteristics are important to you regarding a woman as a *long-term* companion?
28. a) Are you attracted to men? Sexually _____ As friends_____
   b) Why are you attracted to men as you have indicated above?
29. If you had to pick one of the two, which trait in the following groups would you pick characterizing *men in general?* (Underline 1 of the 2 in a,b,c and d)
   a) Dominant or weak   c) Punitive or kind
   b) Warm or cold   d) Loving or not loving
30. Again, if you had to pick one of the two, which trait in the following groups would you pick charcterizing *women in general?* (Follow directions as above.)
   a) Dominant or weak   c) Punitive or kind
   b) Warm or cold   d) Loving or not loving
31. As you look back on your experiences in life what factors do you think were influential in your becoming a lesbian? (Answer fully and use extra sheets if necessary.)
32. If you could relive your life, and if you had a choice, would you become a lesbian? Why or why not?
33. Do you want to change now? If not, please explain.
34. If you do want to change now, what factors are preventing you from doing so?

APPENDIX II

THE ADJECTIVE CHECK LIST AND DEFINITION OF SCALES

The Adjective Check List

by
HARRISON G. GOUGH, Ph.D.
University of California (Berkeley)

Name .... Age .... Sex ....

Date .... Other ....

DIRECTIONS: This booklet contains a list of adjectives. Please read them quickly and put an **X** in the box beside each one you would consider to be self-descriptive. Do not worry about duplications, contradictions, and so forth. Work quickly and do not spend too much time on any one adjective. Try to be frank, and check those adjectives which describe you as you really are, not as you would like to be.

CONSULTING PSYCHOLOGISTS PRESS

577 College Ave., Palo Alto, Calif.

- [ ] absent-minded
  1
- [ ] active
  2
- [ ] adaptable
  3
- [ ] adventurous
  4
- [ ] affected
  5
- [ ] affectionate
  6
- [ ] aggressive
  7
- [ ] alert
  8
- [ ] aloof
  9
- [ ] ambitious
  10
- [ ] anxious
  11
- [ ] apathetic
  12
- [ ] appreciative
  13
- [ ] argumentative
  14
- [ ] arrogant
  15
- [ ] artistic
  16
- [ ] assertive
  17
- [ ] attractive
  18
- [ ] autocratic
  19
- [ ] awkward
  20
- [ ] bitter
  21
- [ ] blustery
  22
- [ ] boastful
  23
- [ ] bossy
  24
- [ ] calm
  25
- [ ] capable
  26
- [ ] careless
  27
- [ ] cautious
  28
- [ ] changeable
  29
- [ ] charming
  30

- [ ] cheerful
  31
- [ ] civilized
  32
- [ ] clear-thinking
  33
- [ ] clever
  34
- [ ] coarse
  35
- [ ] cold
  36
- [ ] commonplace
  37
- [ ] complaining
  38
- [ ] complicated
  39
- [ ] conceited
  40
- [ ] confident
  41
- [ ] confused
  42
- [ ] conscientious
  43
- [ ] conservative
  44
- [ ] considerate
  45
- [ ] contented
  46
- [ ] conventional
  47
- [ ] cool
  48
- [ ] cooperative
  49
- [ ] courageous
  50
- [ ] cowardly
  51
- [ ] cruel
  52
- [ ] curious
  53
- [ ] cynical
  54
- [ ] daring
  55
- [ ] deceitful
  56
- [ ] defensive
  57
- [ ] deliberate
  58
- [ ] demanding
  59
- [ ] dependable
  60

- [ ] dependent
  61
- [ ] despondent
  62
- [ ] determined
  63
- [ ] dignified
  64
- [ ] discreet
  65
- [ ] disorderly
  66
- [ ] dissatisfied
  67
- [ ] distractible
  68
- [ ] distrustful
  69
- [ ] dominant
  70
- [ ] dreamy
  71
- [ ] dull
  72
- [ ] easy going
  73
- [ ] effeminate
  74
- [ ] efficient
  75
- [ ] egotistical
  76
- [ ] emotional
  77
- [ ] energetic
  78
- [ ] enterprising
  79
- [ ] enthusiastic
  80
- [ ] evasive
  81
- [ ] excitable
  82
- [ ] fair-minded
  83
- [ ] fault-finding
  84
- [ ] fearful
  85
- [ ] feminine
  86
- [ ] fickle
  87
- [ ] flirtatious
  88
- [ ] foolish
  89
- [ ] forceful
  90

- [ ] foresighted
  91
- [ ] forgetful
  92
- [ ] forgiving
  93
- [ ] formal
  94
- [ ] frank
  95
- [ ] friendly
  96
- [ ] frivolous
  97
- [ ] fussy
  98
- [ ] generous
  99
- [ ] gentle
  100
- [ ] gloomy
  101
- [ ] good-looking
  102
- [ ] good-natured
  103
- [ ] greedy
  104
- [ ] handsome
  105
- [ ] hard-headed
  106
- [ ] hard-hearted
  107
- [ ] hasty
  108
- [ ] headstrong
  109
- [ ] healthy
  110
- [ ] helpful
  111
- [ ] high-strung
  112
- [ ] honest
  113
- [ ] hostile
  114
- [ ] humorous
  115
- [ ] hurried
  116
- [ ] idealistic
  117
- [ ] imaginative
  118
- [ ] immature
  119
- [ ] impatient
  120

- [ ] impulsive
  121
- [ ] independent
  122
- [ ] indifferent
  123
- [ ] individualistic
  124
- [ ] industrious
  125
- [ ] infantile
  126
- [ ] informal
  127
- [ ] ingenious
  128
- [ ] inhibited
  129
- [ ] initiative
  130
- [ ] insightful
  131
- [ ] intelligent
  132
- [ ] interests narrow
  133
- [ ] interests wide
  134
- [ ] intolerant
  135
- [ ] inventive
  136
- [ ] irresponsible
  137
- [ ] irritable
  138
- [ ] jolly
  139
- [ ] kind
  140
- [ ] lazy
  141
- [ ] leisurely
  142
- [ ] logical
  143
- [ ] loud
  144
- [ ] loyal
  145
- [ ] mannerly
  146
- [ ] masculine
  147
- [ ] mature
  148
- [ ] meek
  149
- [ ] methodical
  150

DO NOT WRITE B

+												
−												

☐ mild
151

☐ mischievous
152

☐ moderate
153

☐ modest
154

☐ moody
155

☐ nagging
156

☐ natural
157

☐ nervous
158

☐ noisy
159

☐ obliging
160

☐ obnoxious
161

☐ opinionated
162

☐ opportunistic
163

☐ optimistic
164

☐ organized
165

☐ original
166

☐ outgoing
167

☐ outspoken
168

☐ painstaking
169

☐ patient
170

☐ peaceable
171

☐ peculiar
172

☐ persevering
173

☐ persistent
174

☐ pessimistic
175

☐ planful
176

☐ pleasant
177

☐ pleasure-seeking
178

☐ poised
179

☐ polished
180

☐ practical
181

☐ praising
182

☐ precise
183

☐ prejudiced
184

☐ preoccupied
185

☐ progressive
186

☐ prudish
187

☐ quarrelsome
188

☐ queer
189

☐ quick
190

☐ quiet
191

☐ quitting
192

☐ rational
193

☐ rattlebrained
194

☐ realistic
195

☐ reasonable
196

☐ rebellious
197

☐ reckless
198

☐ reflective
199

☐ relaxed
200

☐ reliable
201

☐ resentful
202

☐ reserved
203

☐ resourceful
204

☐ responsible
205

☐ restless
206

☐ retiring
207

☐ rigid
208

☐ robust
209

☐ rude
210

☐ sarcastic
211

☐ self-centered
212

☐ self-confident
213

☐ self-controlled
214

☐ self-denying
215

☐ self-pitying
216

☐ self-punishing
217

☐ self-seeking
218

☐ selfish
219

☐ sensitive
220

☐ sentimental
221

☐ serious
222

☐ severe
223

☐ sexy
224

☐ shallow
225

☐ sharp-witted
226

☐ shiftless
227

☐ show-off
228

☐ shrewd
229

☐ shy
230

☐ silent
231

☐ simple
232

☐ sincere
233

☐ slipshod
234

☐ slow
235

☐ sly
236

☐ smug
237

☐ snobbish
238

☐ sociable
239

☐ soft-hearted
240

☐ sophisticated
241

☐ spendthrift
242

☐ spineless
243

☐ spontaneous
244

☐ spunky
245

☐ stable
246

☐ steady
247

☐ stern
248

☐ stingy
249

☐ stolid
250

☐ strong
251

☐ stubborn
252

☐ submissive
253

☐ suggestible
254

☐ sulky
255

☐ superstitious
256

☐ suspicious
257

☐ sympathetic
258

☐ tactful
259

☐ tactless
260

☐ talkative
261

☐ temperamental
262

☐ tense
263

☐ thankless
264

☐ thorough
265

☐ thoughtful
266

☐ thrifty
267

☐ timid
268

☐ tolerant
269

☐ touchy
270

☐ tough
271

☐ trusting
272

☐ unaffected
273

☐ unambitious
274

☐ unassuming
275

☐ unconventional
276

☐ undependable
277

☐ understanding
278

☐ unemotional
279

☐ unexcitable
280

☐ unfriendly
281

☐ uninhibited
282

☐ unintelligent
283

☐ unkind
284

☐ unrealistic
285

☐ unscrupulous
286

☐ unselfish
287

☐ unstable
288

☐ vindictive
289

☐ versatile
290

☐ warm
291

☐ wary
292

☐ weak
293

☐ whiny
294

☐ wholesome
295

☐ wise
296

☐ withdrawn
297

☐ witty
298

☐ worrying
299

☐ zany
300

ELOW THIS LINE

ADJECTIVE CHECK LIST
DEFINITION OF SCALES

Designation on profile sheet	Name
1. No. Ckd	Total number of adjectives checked
2. Df	Defensiveness
3. Fav	Number of favorable adjectives checked
4. Unfav	Number of unfavorable adjectives checked
5. S-Cfd	Self-confidence
6. S-Cn	Self-control
7. Lab	Lability
8. Per Adj	Personal adjustment

The Need Scales

9. Ach	Achievement: to strive to be outstanding in pursuits of socially recognized significance.
10. Dom	Dominance: to seek and sustain leadership roles in groups or to be influential and controlling in individual relationships.
11. End	Endurance: to persist in any task undertaken.
12. Ord	Order: to place special emphasis on neatness, organization, and planning in one's activities.
13. Int	Intraception: to engage in attempts to understand one's own behavior or the behavior of others.
14. Nur	Nurturance: to engage in behaviors which extend material or emotional benefits to others.
15. Aff	Affiliation: to seek and sustain numerous personal friendships.
16. Het	Heterosexuality: to seek the company of and derive emotional satisfactions from interactions with opposite-sexed peers.

17. Exh	Exhibition: To behave in such a way as to elicit the immediate attention of others.
18. Aut	Autonomy: to act independently of others or of social values and expectations.
19. Agg	Aggression: to engage in behaviors which attack or hurt others.
20. Cha	Change: to seek novelty of experience and avoid routine.
21. Suc	Succorance: to solicit sympathy, affection, or emotional support from others.
22. Aba	Abasement: to express feelings of inferiority through self-criticism, guilt, or social impotence.
23. Def	Deference: to seek and sustain subordinate roles in relationships with others.
24. Crs	Counseling readiness

APPENDIX III

INDIVIDUAL ADJECTIVE CHECK LIST PROFILES

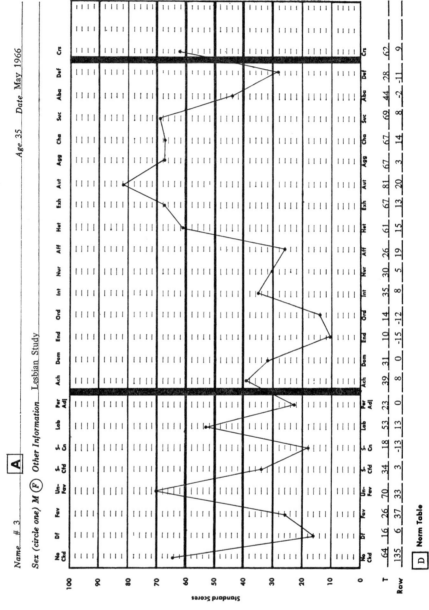

PROFILE SHEET FOR THE ADJECTIVE CHECK LIST

Name # 3   Age 35   Date May 1966

A

Sex (circle one) M (F)   Other Information   Lesbian Study

D   Norm Table

	No Ckd	Df	Fav	Un-Fav	S-Ckd	S-Cn	Lab	Per Adj	Ach	Dom	End	Ord	Int	Nur	Aff	Het	Exh	Aut	Agg	Cha	Suc	Aba	Def	Crs
T	64	16	26	70	34	18	53	23	39	31	10	14	35	30	26	61	67	81	67	67	69	44	28	62
Raw	135	6	37	33	3	-13	13	0	8	0	-15	-12	8	5	19	15	13	20	3	14	8	-2	-11	9

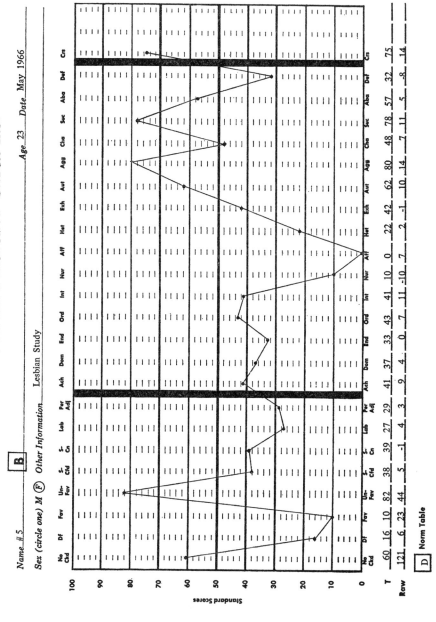

PROFILE SHEET FOR THE ADJECTIVE CHECK LIST

Name _#11_   Age _20_ Date _May 1966_

Sex (circle one) M (F) Other Information _Lesbian Study_

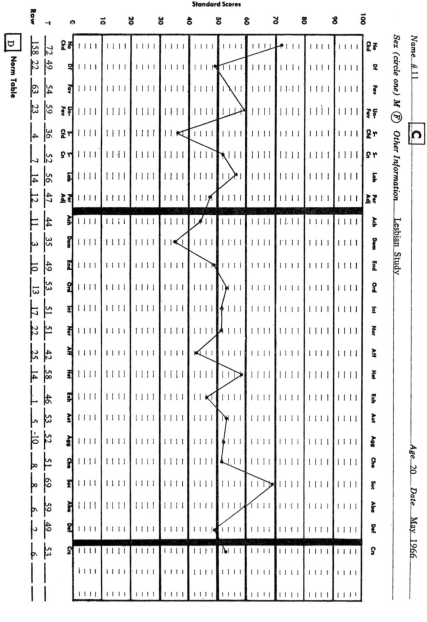

	No Ckd	Df	Fav	Un-Fav	Com Ckd	Com Cn	Lab	Per Adj	Ach	Dom	End	Ord	Int	Nur	Aff	Het	Exh	Aut	Agg	Cha	Suc	Aba	Def	Crs
T	72	49	54	59	36	52	56	47	44	35	49	53	51	51	42	58	46	53	52	51	69	59	49	53
Raw	158	22	63	23	4	7	14	12	7	3	10	13	17	22	25	14	1	5	-10	8	8	6	2	6

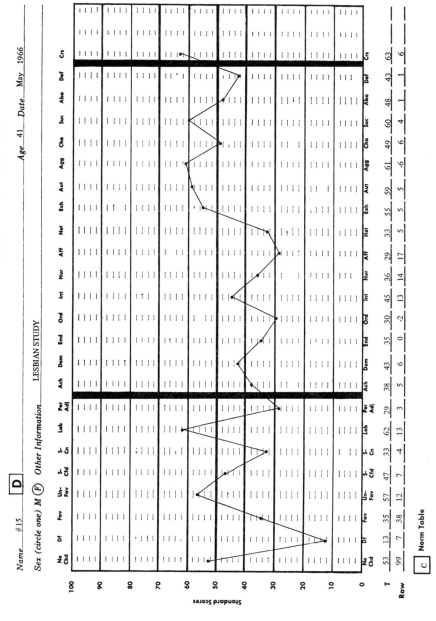

PROFILE SHEET FOR THE ADJECTIVE CHECK LIST

Name #15   D   Age 41   Date May 1966

Sex (circle one) M (F)   Other Information   LESBIAN STUDY

	No Ckd	Df	Fav	Un-Fav	S-Cfd	S-Cn	Lab	Per Adj	Ach	Dom	End	Ord	Int	Nur	Aff	Het	Exh	Aut	Agg	Cha	Suc	Aba	Def	Crs
T	53	13	35	57	47	33	62	29	38	43	35	30	45	36	29	33	55	59	61	49	60	48	43	63
Raw	99	7	38	12	7	-4	13	3	5	6	0	-2	13	14	17	5	5	5	-6	6	4	1	1	6

C   Norm Table

PROFILE SHEET FOR THE ADJECTIVE CHECK LIST

E

Name #16   *Age* 22   *Date* May 1966

Sex (circle one) M (F)   *Other Information* Lesbian Study

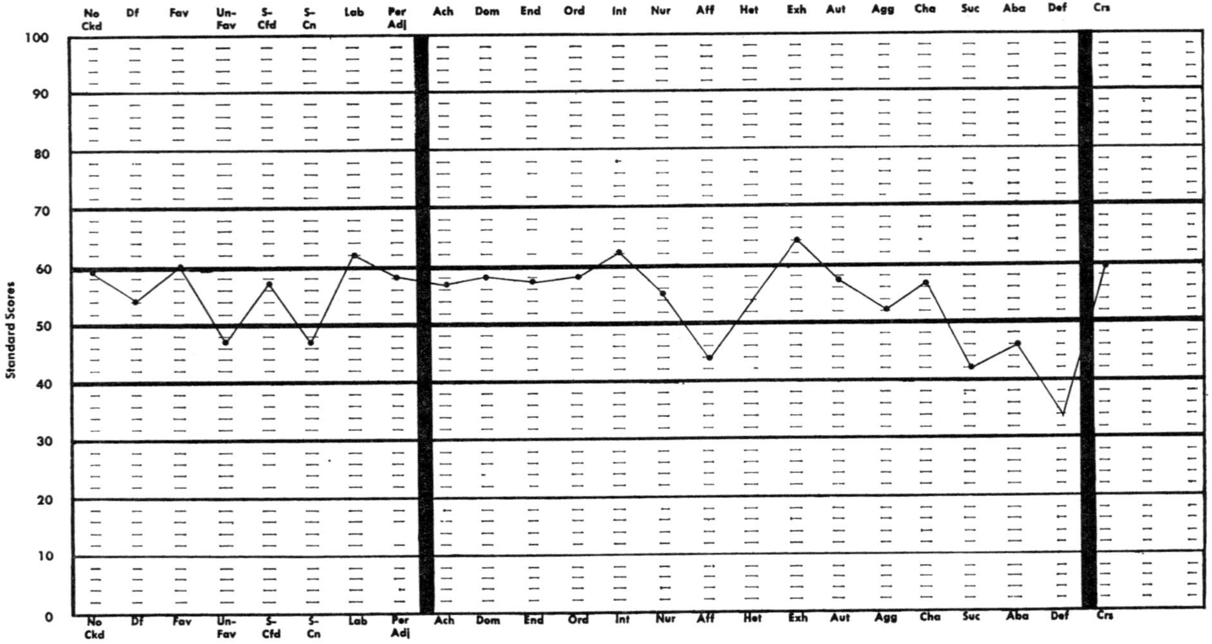

	No Ckd	Df	Fav	Un- Fav	S- Cfd	S- Cn	Lab	Per Adj	Ach	Dom	End	Ord	Int	Nur	Aff	Het	Exh	Aut	Agg	Cha	Suc	Aba	Def	Crs
T	59	54	60	47	57	47	62	58	57	58	57	58	62	55	44	54	64	57	52	57	42	46	34	60
Raw	119	24	60	6	12	4	13	16	15	16	13	13	19	26	23	12	10	4	13	9	2	0	4	5

Standard Scores

C Norm Table

PROFILE SHEET FOR THE ADJECTIVE CHECK LIST

Name #24   Age 43   Date May 1966

Sex (circle one) M (F)   Other Information LESBIAN STUDY

	No Ckd	Df	Fav	Un- Fav	S- Ckd	S- Cn	Lab	Per Adj	Ach	Dom	End	Ord	Int	Nur	Aff	Het	Exh	Aut	Agg	Cha	Suc	Aba	Def	Crs
T	68	55	63	37	55	63	56	65	61	59	60	61	58	59	57	61	49	42	47	46	36	48	53	51
Raw	147	25	71	2	14	13	14	21	20	19	17	18	21	28	31	15	3	-1	-15	6	-4	0	5	5

D Norm Table

PROFILE SHEET FOR THE ADJECTIVE CHECK LIST

Name #25 　　　G　　　　Age 34　Date May 1966

Sex (circle one) M (F)　Other Information　Lesbian Study

	No Chd	Df	Fav	Un-Fav	S-Cfd	S-Cn	Lab	Per Adj	Ach	Dom	End	Ord	Int	Nur	Aff	Het	Exh	Aut	Agg	Cha	Suc	Aba	Def	Crs
T	78	53	58	59	66	44	59	45	54	50	41	40	51	53	42	49	56	64	52	48	53	48	42	56
Raw	178	24	66	23	20	2	15	11	16	13	5	5	17	23	25	11	7	11	-10	7	2	0	-2	7

D　Norm Table

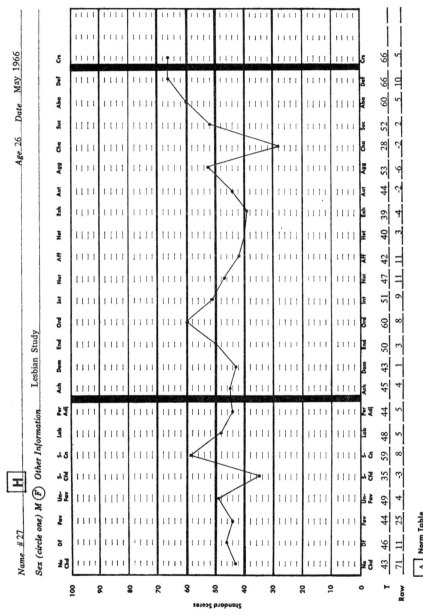

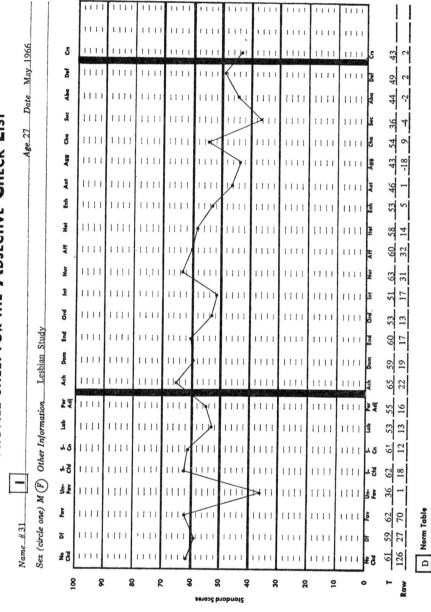

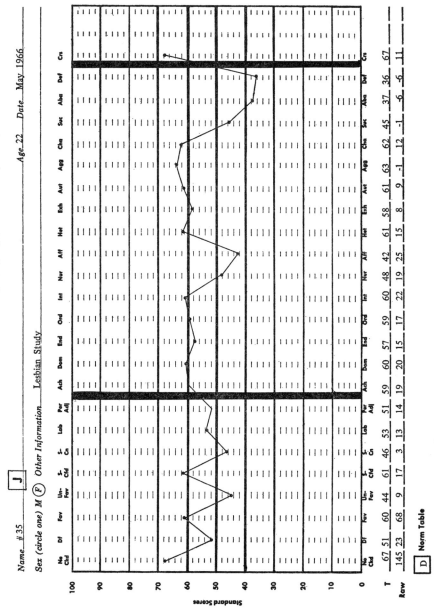

PROFILE SHEET FOR THE **A**DJECTIVE **C**HECK **L**IST

Name #35   J   Age 22   Date May 1966

Sex (circle one) M (F)   Other Information   Lesbian Study

D   Norm Table

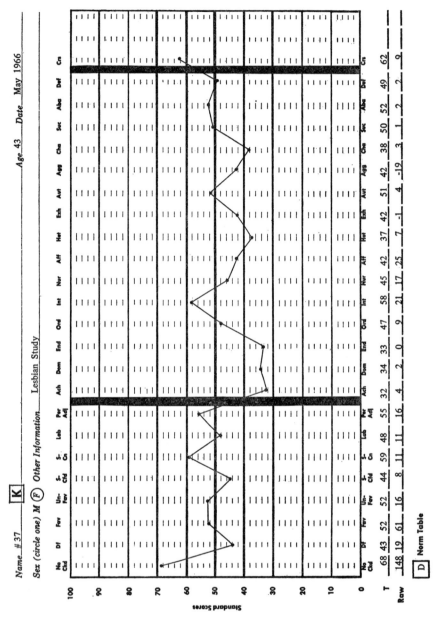

PROFILE SHEET FOR THE ADJECTIVE CHECK LIST

Name #37   K   Age 43   Date May 1966

Sex (circle one) M (F)   Other Information   Lesbian Study

	No Ckd	Df	Fav	Un-Fav	S-Cfd	S-Cn	Lab	Per Adj	Ach	Dom	End	Ord	Int	Nur	Aff	Het	Exh	Aut	Agg	Cha	Suc	Aba	Def	Crs
T	68	43	52	52	44	59	48	55	32	34	33	47	58	45	42	37	42	51	42	38	50	52	49	62
Raw	148	19	61	16	8	11	11	16	4	2	0	9	21	17	25	7	-1	4	-19	3	1	2	2	9

D Norm Table

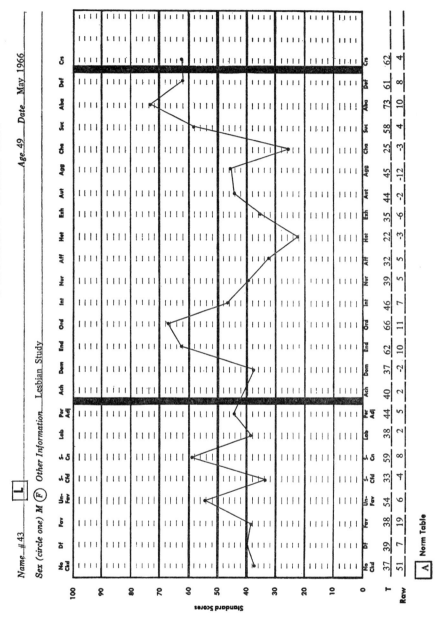

PROFILE SHEET FOR THE **ADJECTIVE CHECK LIST**

Name. # 43   Age. 49   Date. May 1966

Sex (circle one) M (F)   Other Information. Lesbian Study

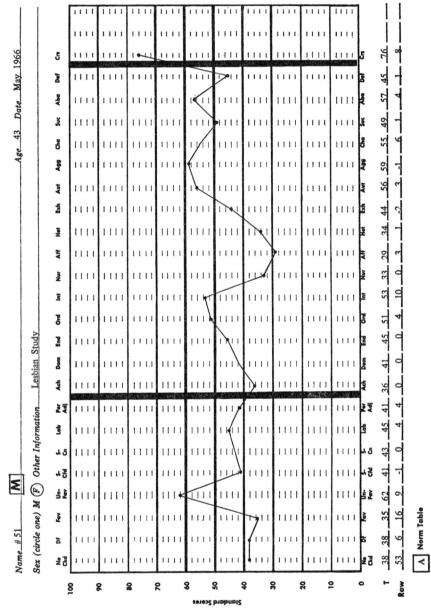

PROFILE SHEET FOR THE **ADJECTIVE CHECK LIST**

Name: #51   M   Age 43 Date May 1966

Sex (circle one) M Ⓕ   Other Information Lesbian Study

A   Norm Table

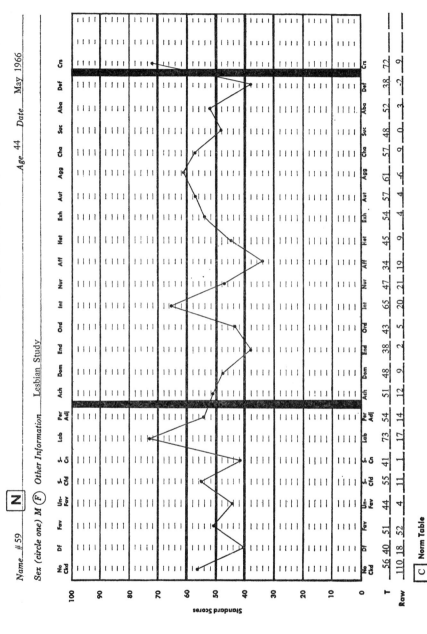

PROFILE SHEET FOR THE ADJECTIVE CHECK LIST

Name #60   □ O   Age 22   Date May 1966

Sex (circle one) M Ⓕ Other Information Lesbian Study

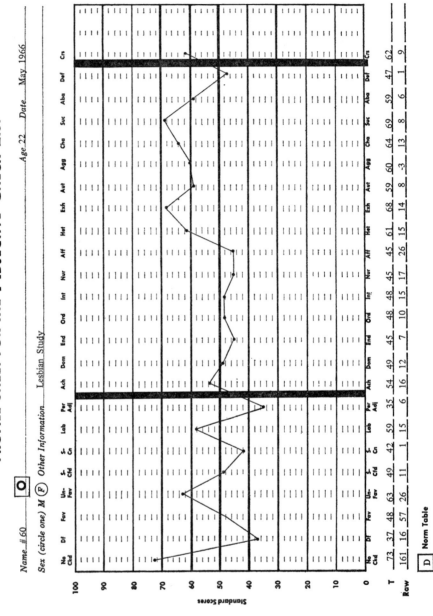

	No Ckd	Df	Fav	Un- Fav	S- Ckd	S- Cn	Lab	Per Adj	Ach	Dom	End	Ord	Int	Nur	Aff	Het	Exh	Aut	Agg	Cha	Suc	Aba	Def	Crs
T	73	37	48	63	49	42	59	35	54	49	45	48	48	45	45	61	68	59	60	64	69	59	47	62
Raw	161	16	57	26	11	1	15	6	16	12	7	10	15	17	26	15	14	8	-3	13	8	6	1	9

D Norm Table

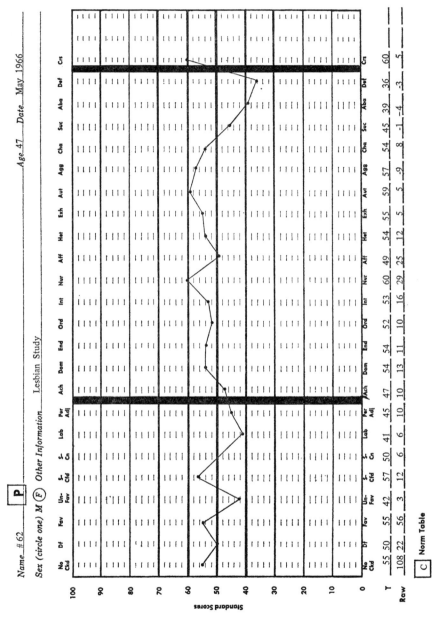

PROFILE SHEET FOR THE ADJECTIVE CHECK LIST

Name #62   Age 47   Date May 1966

Sex (circle one) M (F)   Other Information   Lesbian Study

Standard Scores

	No Ckd	Df	Fav	Un-Fav	S-Cfd	S-Cn	Lab	Per Adj	Ach	Dom	End	Ord	Int	Nur	Aff	Het	Exh	Aut	Agg	Cha	Suc	Aba	Def	Crs
T	55	50	55	42	57	50	41	45	47	54	54	52	53	60	49	54	55	59	57	54	45	39	36	60
Raw	108	22	56	3	12	6	6	10	10	13	11	10	16	29	25	12	5	5	-9	8	-1	-4	-3	5

C   Norm Table

PROFILE SHEET FOR THE **ADJECTIVE CHECK LIST**

Name #64   Q

Sex (circle one) M F   Other Information   Lesbian Study

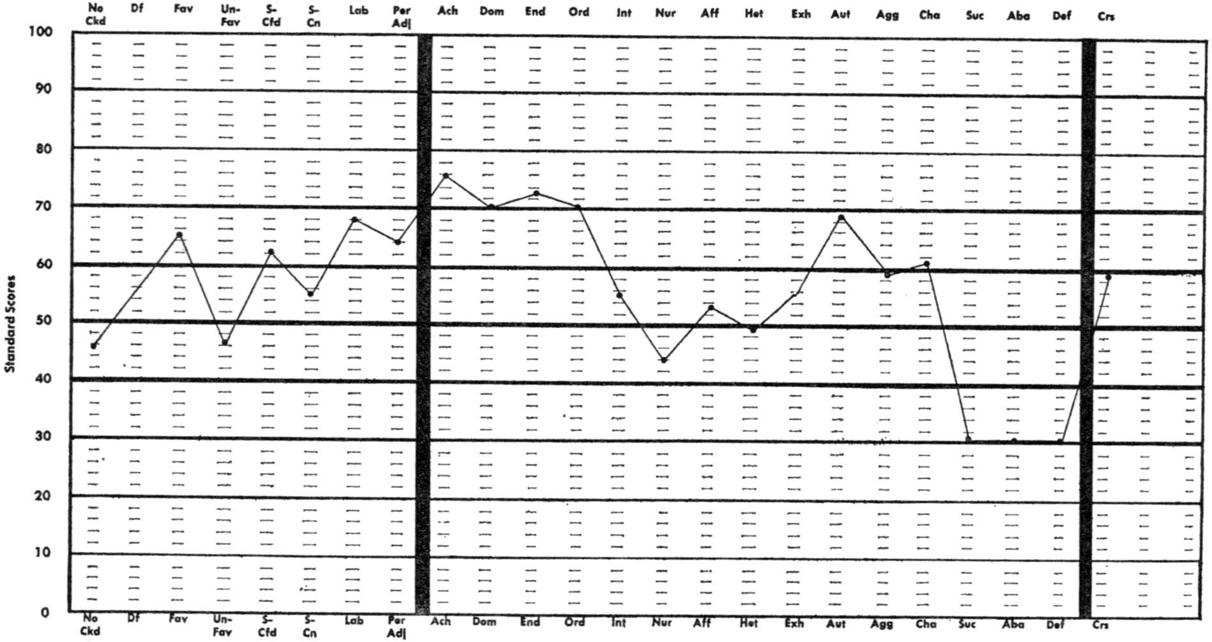

Age 40   Date May 1966

Standard Scores

	No Ckd	Df	Fav	Un-Fav	S-Cfd	S-Cn	Lab	Per Adj	Ach	Dom	End	Ord	Int	Nur	Aff	Het	Exh	Aut	Agg	Cha	Suc	Aba	Def	Crs
T	45	54	65	46	62	55	68	64	76	70	73	70	55	44	53	49	56	69	59	61	30	30	30	59
Raw	77	16	44	3	8	6	11	13	17	16	16	13	11	9	17	6	3	8	-1	8	-5	-6	-6	3

A   Norm Table

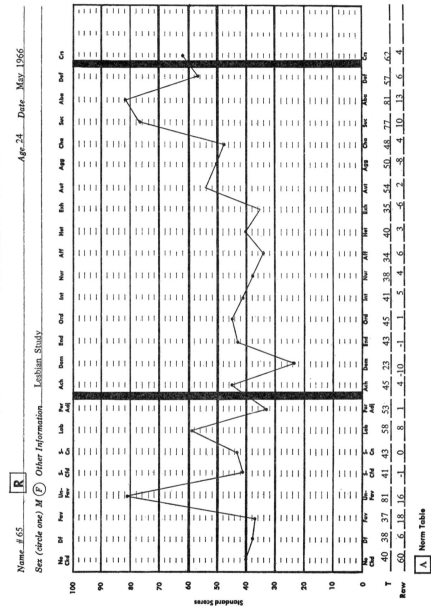

PROFILE SHEET FOR THE ADJECTIVE CHECK LIST

Name #65   R   Age 24   Date May 1966

Sex (circle one) M (F)   Other Information   Lesbian Study

A Norm Table

	No Chd	Df	Fav	Un-Fav	S-Cfd	S-Cn	Lab	Per Adj	Ach	Dom	End	Ord	Int	Nur	Aff	Het	Exh	Aut	Agg	Cha	Suc	Aba	Def	Crs
T	40	38	37	81	41	43	58	53	45	23	43	45	41	38	34	40	35	54	50	48	77	81	57	62
Raw	60	6	18	16	-1	0	8	1	4	-10	-1	1	5	4	6	3	-6	2	-8	4	10	13	6	4

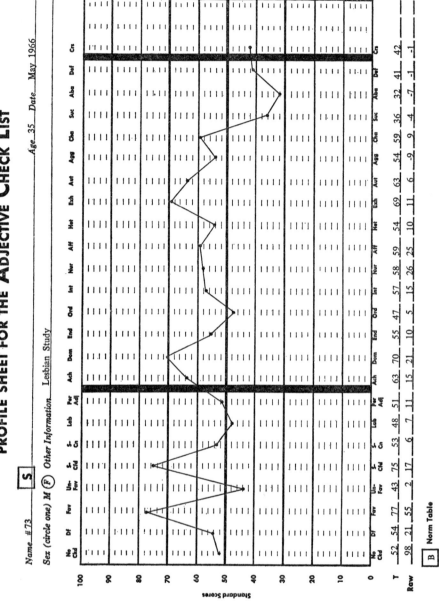

PROFILE SHEET FOR THE **A**DJECTIVE **C**HECK **L**IST

Name #73   Age 35 Date May 1966

Sex (circle one) M Ⓕ Other Information Lesbian Study

	No Ckd	Df	Fav	Un-Fav	S-Ckd	S-Cn	Lab	Per Adj	Ach	Dom	End	Ord	Int	Nur	Aff	Het	Exh	Aut	Agg	Cha	Suc	Aba	Def	Crs
T	52	54	77	43	75	53	48	51	63	70	55	47	57	58	59	54	69	63	54	59	36	32	41	42
Raw	98	21	55	2	17	6	7	11	15	21	10	5	15	26	25	10	11	6	-9	9	4	-7	-1	-1

B Norm Table

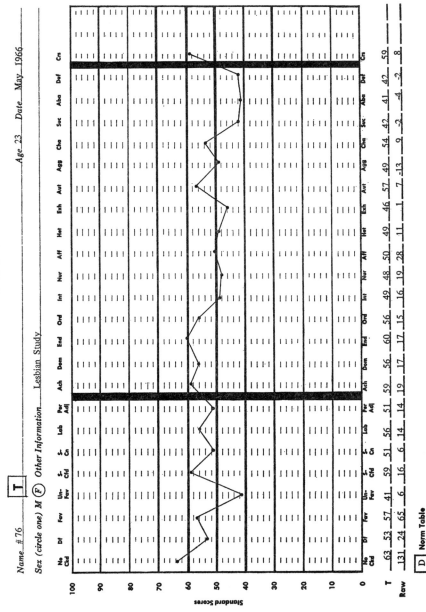

PROFILE SHEET FOR THE ADJECTIVE CHECK LIST

Name #76   Age 23   Date May 1966

Sex (circle one) M Ⓕ Other Information   Lesbian Study

	No Ckd	Df	Fav	Un-Fav	S-Cfd	S-Cn	Per Adj	Ach	Dom	End	Ord	Int	Nur	Aff	Het	Exh	Aut	Agg	Cha	Suc	Aba	Def	Crs
T	63	53	57	41	59	51	51	59	56	60	56	49	48	50	49	46	57	49	54	42	41	42	59
Raw	131	24	65	6	16	6	14	19	17	17	15	16	19	28	11	-1	7	-13	9	-2	-4	-2	8

D Norm Table

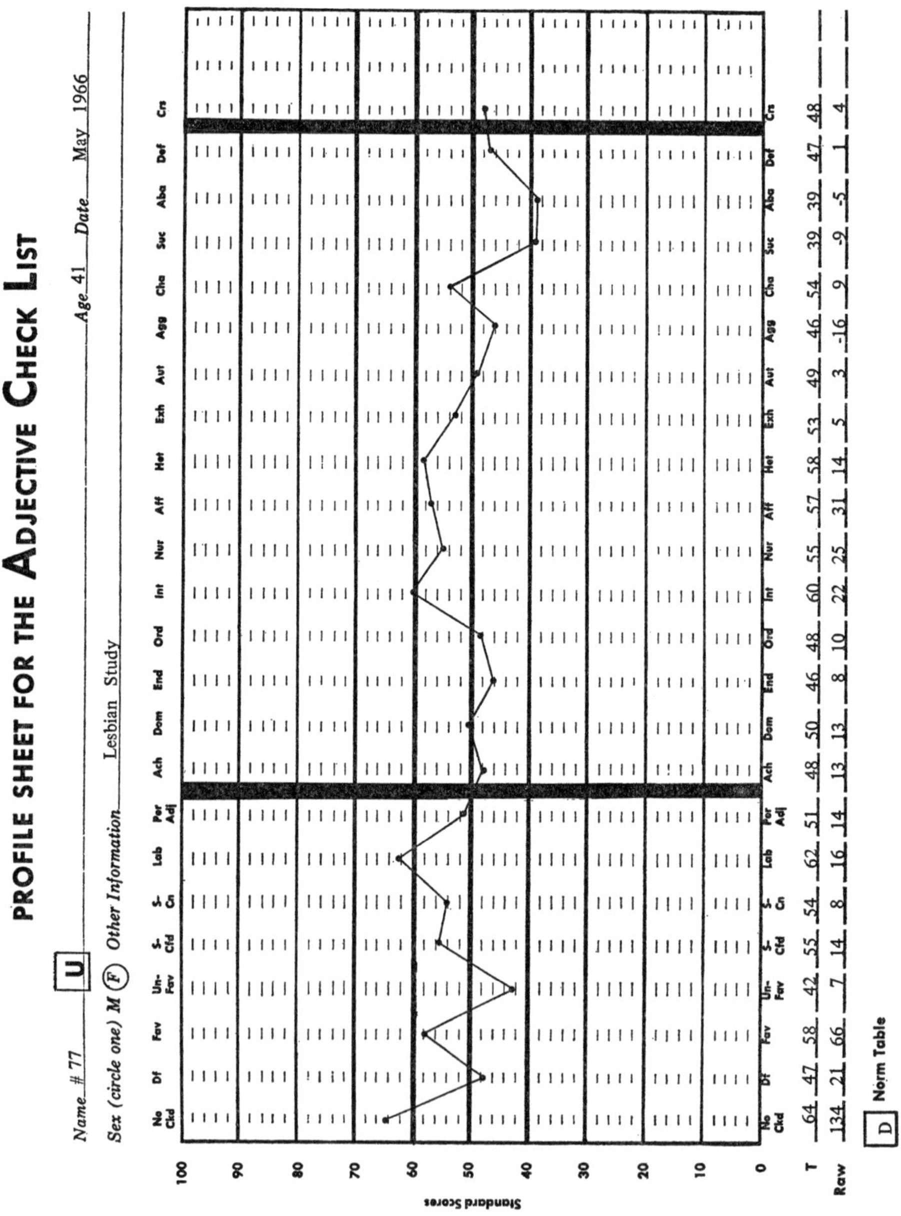

PROFILE SHEET FOR THE ADJECTIVE CHECK LIST

Name # 77   U   Age 41   Date May 1966

Sex (circle one) M (F)   Other Information   Lesbian Study

	No Ckd	Df	Fav	Un-Fav	S-Cfd	S-Cn	Lab	Per Adj	Ach	Dom	End	Ord	Int	Nur	Aff	Het	Exh	Aut	Agg	Cha	Suc	Aba	Def	Crs
T	64	47	58	42	55	54	62	51	48	50	46	48	60	55	57	58	53	49	46	54	39	39	47	48
Raw	134	21	66	7	14	8	16	14	13	13	8	10	22	25	31	14	5	3	-16	9	-9	-5	1	4

Standard Scores

D Norm Table

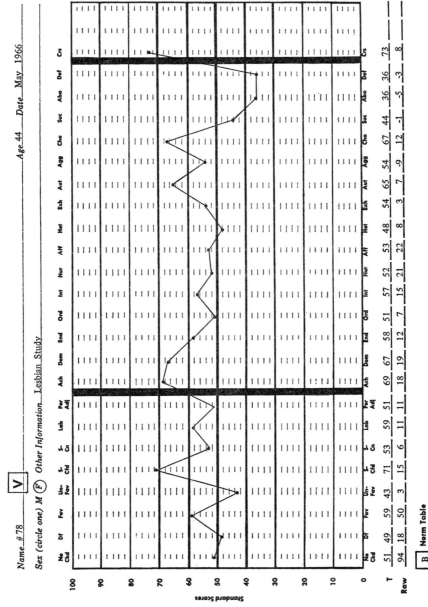

PROFILE SHEET FOR THE ADJECTIVE CHECK LIST

Name #78   [V]   Age 44   Date May 1966

Sex (circle one) M (F)   Other Information Lesbian Study

	No Ckd	Df	Fav	Un-Fav	S-Cfd	S-Cn	Lab	Per Adj	Ach	Dom	End	Ord	Int	Nur	Aff	Het	Exh	Aut	Agg	Cha	Suc	Aba	Def	Crs
T	51	49	59	43	71	53	59	51	69	67	58	51	57	52	53	48	54	65	54	67	44	36	36	73
Raw	94	18	50	3	15	6	11	11	18	19	12	7	15	21	22	8	3	7	-9	12	-1	-5	-3	8

[B] Norm Table

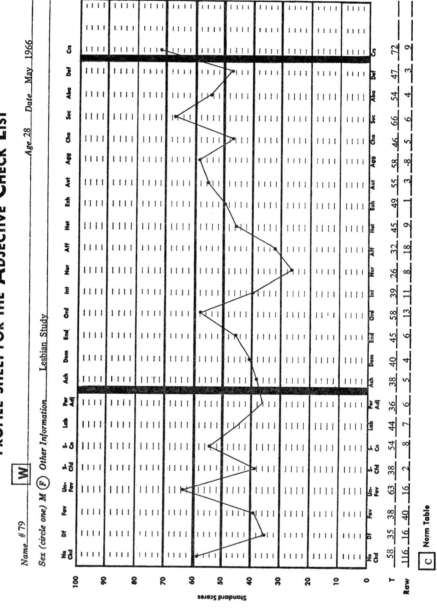

PROFILE SHEET FOR THE ADJECTIVE CHECK LIST

Name. #79   W

Sex (circle one) M (F) Other Information   Lesbian Study

Age 28   Date May 1966

	No Ckd	Df	Few	Un-Fav	S-Cfd	S-Cn	Lab	Per Adj	Ach	Dom	End	Ord	Int	Nur	Aff	Het	Exh	Aut	Agg	Cha	Suc	Aba	Def	Cs
T	58	35	38	63	38	54	44	36	38	40	45	58	39	26	32	45	49	55	58	46	66	54	47	72
Raw	116	16	40	16	2	8	7	6	5	4	6	13	11	8	18	9	1	3	-8	5	6	4	3	9

C Norm Table

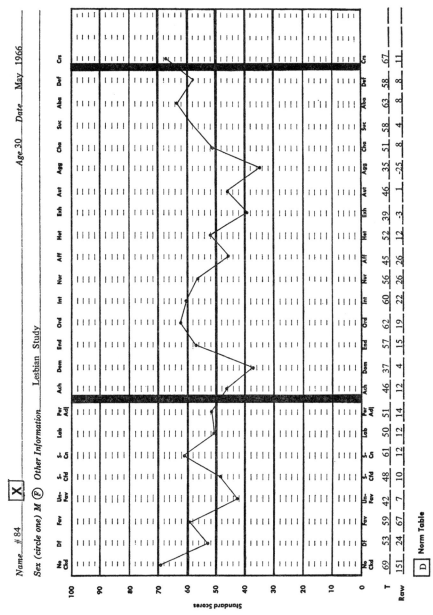

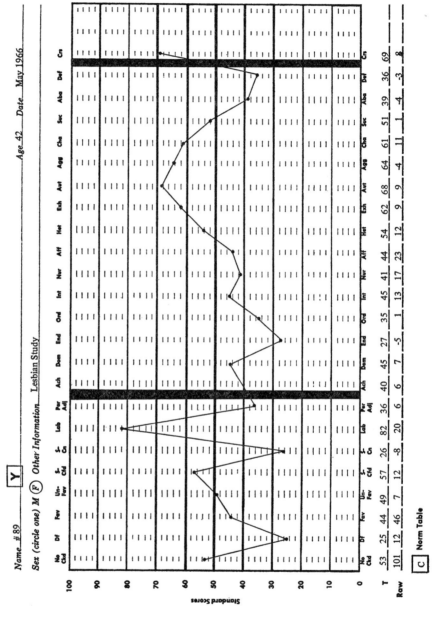

PROFILE SHEET FOR THE ADJECTIVE CHECK LIST

Name __#97__   Age __38__ Date __May 1966__

Sex (circle one) M (F) Other Information __Lesbian Study__

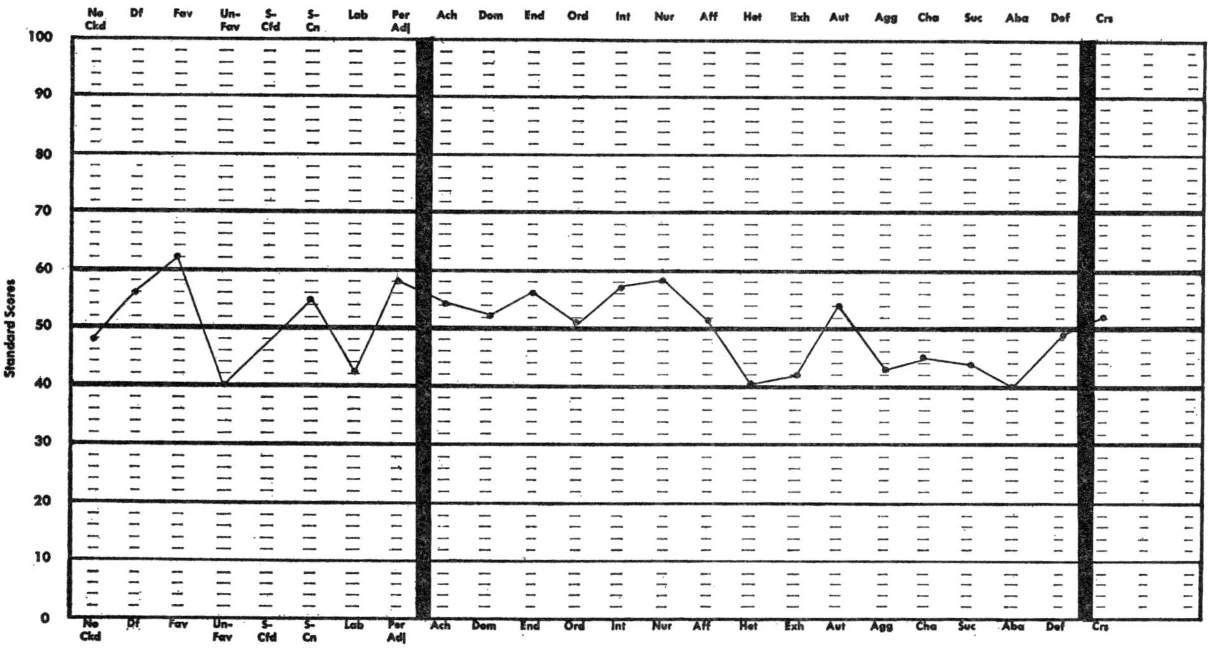

Z

	No Ckd	Df	Fav	Un-Fav	S-Cfd	S-Ctd	Lab	Per Adj	Ach	Dom	End	Ord	Int	Nur	Aff	Het	Exh	Aut	Agg	Cha	Suc	Aba	Def	Crs
T	48	56	62	40	47	55	42	58	54	52	56	51	57	58	51	40	42	54	43	45	44	40	49	52
Raw	85	22	52	1	4	7	5	14	11	10	11	7	15	26	21	5	4	2	-18	4	-1	-3	-4	2

B Norm Table

Standard Scores: 100, 90, 80, 70, 60, 50, 40, 30, 20, 10, 0

BIBLIOGRAPHY

Armon, V.: Some personality variables in overt female homosexuality. *J Proj Tech Pers Asses, 24*:292-309, 1960.

Asimos, C., and Rosen, D. H.: *Suicide and Homosexuality;* unpublished manuscript.

Auerback, A. E.: Understanding sexual deviations. *Postgrad Med, 43*(2): 125-129; *43*(3):169-173, 1968.

Bacon, C. L.: A developmental theory of female homosexuality. In Lorand, S. (Ed.): *Preversions: Psychodynamics and Therapy.* New York, Random House, 1956, 131-159.

Beach, F. A.: Sexual behavior in animals and men. *Harvey Lecture Series, 43*:254-280, 1948.

Bene, E.: On the genesis of female homosexuality. *Br J Psychiatry, 111*:815-821, 1965.

Bergler, E.: *Neurotic Counterfeit-Sex.* New York, Grune and Stratton, 1951.

Boston Women's Health Book Collective: *Our Bodies, Ourselves.* New York, Simon and Schuster, 1973.

British Medical Association: *Homosexuality and Prostitution.* London, Fisher, Knight and Co., 1955.

Cory, D. W.: *The Lesbian in America.* New York, Citadel Pr, 1964.

Capiro, F. S.: *Female Homosexuality: A Psychodynamic Study of Lesbianism.* New York, Citadel Pr, 1954.

de Saussure, R.: Homosexual fixations in neurotic women. *Rev Fran Psychanal, 3*:50-91, 1929.

Deutsch, H.: On female homosexuality (1932). In *The Psychoanalytic Reader,* Vol. 1. New York, International Universities Press, 1948, 237-260.

Fenichel, O.: *The Psychoanalytic Theory of Neurosis.* New York, Norton, 1945.

Freedman, M. J.: Homosexuality among women and psychological adjustment. *Ladder, 12*:2-3, 1968.

Freud, S.: Letter to an American mother. *Am J Psychiatry, 107*:786-787, 1951.

Freud, S.: The psychogenesis of a case of homosexuality in a woman (1920). In *The Collected Papers,* Vol. II. London, Hogarth, 1948, 202-231.

Freud, S.: The psychology of women. In *New Introductory Lectures on Psyco-analysis.* New York, Norton, 1933, 153-185.

Gough, H. G., and Heilbrun, A. B., Jr.: *The Adjective Check List Manual.* Palo Alto, Consulting Psychologists Press, 1965.

Gundlach, R. H.: Childhood parental relationships and the establishment of gender roles of homosexuals. *J Consult Clin Psychol, 33*:136-139, 1969.

Gundlach, R. H., and Riess, B. F.: Self and sexual identity in the female: A study of female homosexuals. In Riess, B. F. (Ed.): *New Directions in Mental Health,* Vol. 1. New York, Grune and Stratton, 1968, 205-231.

Henry, G. W.: *Sex Variants: A Study of Homosexual Patterns.* New York, Hoeber, 1948.

Hopkins, J. H.: The lesbian personality. *Br J Psychiatry, 115:*1433-1436, 1969.

Horney, K.: The flight from womanhood: The masculinity complex in women, as viewed by men and by women. *Int J Psychoanal, 7:*324-339, 1926.

Hospital Tribune, August 21, 1972.

Jones, E.: The early development of female sexuality. *Int J Psychoanal, 8:* 459-472, 1927.

Kaye, H. E.: Lesbian relationships. *Sexual Behavior,* April, 1971, 80-87.

Kaye, H. E., Berl, S., Clare, J., *et al.:* Homosexuality in women. *Arch Gen Psychiatry, 17:*626-634, 1967.

Kenyon, F. E.: Studies in female homosexuality—psychological test results. *J Consult Clin Psychol, 32:*510-513, 1968a.

Kenyon, F. E.: Studies in female homosexuality. IV. Social and psychiatric aspects. *Br J Psychiatry, 114:*1337-1350, 1968b.

Kinsey, A. C., Pomeroy, W. B., Martin, C. E., and Gebhard, D. H.: *Sexual Behavior in the Human Female.* Philadelphia, Saunders, 1953.

Loney, J.: Background factors, sexual experiences, and attitudes toward treatment in two "normal" homosexual samples. *J Consult Clin Psychol, 38:*57-65, 1972.

Loraine, J. A., Adampopoulos, D. A., Kirkham, K. E., Ismail, A .A. A., and Dove, G. A.: Patterns of hormone excretion in male and female homosexuals. *Nature, 234:*552-554, 1971.

Lyon, P., and Martin, D.: *Lesbian/Woman.* San Francisco, Glide Urban Ctr, 1972.

Marmor, J.: *Sexual Inversion. The Multiple Roots of Homosexuality.* New York, Basic Books, 1965.

Menninger, K.: quoted in *Psychiatric News,* January 17, 1973, *8:*2.

Perloff, W. H.: Hormones and homosexuality. In Marmor, J. (Ed.): *Sexual Inversion. The Multiple Roots of Homosexuality.* New York, Basic Books, 1965, 44-69.

Radio, S.: Fear of castration in women. *Psychoanal Quart, 2:*425-475, 1933.

Romm, M. E.: Sexuality and homosexuality in women. In Marmor, J. (Ed.): *Sexual Inversion. The Multiple Roots of Homosexuality.* New York, Basic Books, 1965, 282-301.

Saghir, M. R., and Robins, E.: Male and female homosexuality: Natural history. *Compr Psychiatry, 12:*503-510, 1971.

Siegelman, M.: Adjustment of homosexual and heterosexual women. *Br J Psychiatry, 120:*477-481, 1972.

Simon, W., and Gagnon, J. H.: Femininity in the lesbian community. *Social Prob, 15*:212-221, 1967.

Socarides, C. W.: The historical development of theoretical and clinical concepts of overt female homosexuality. *J Am Psychoanal Ass, 11*:386-414, 1963.

Socarides, C. W.: *The Overt Homosexual.* New York, Grune and Stratton, 1968.

Swanson, D. W., Loomis, S. D. and Lukesh, R., *et al.:* Clinical features of the female homosexual patient. *J. Nerv. Ment. Dis., 155*:119-124, 1972.

Szasz, T. S.: Legal and moral aspects of homosexuality. In Marmor, J. (Ed.): *Sexual Inversion. The Multiple Roots of Homosexuality.* New York, Basic Books, 1965, 124-139.

This World, San Francisco Sunday Examiner and Chronicle, Lesbians win child custody. February 25, 1973, p. 6.

Thompson, N. D., McCandless, B. R., and Strickland, B. R.: Personal adjustment of male and female homosexuals and heterosexuals. *J Abnorm Psychol, 78*:237-240, 1971.

Wilbur, C. B.: Clinical aspects of female homosexuality. In Marmor, J. (Ed.): *Sexual Inversion. The Multiple Roots of Homosexuality.* New York, Basic Books, 1965, 268-281.

Wolff, C.: *Love Between Women.* New York, St Martin, 1972.

Wortis, J.: *Fragments of An Analysis with Freud.* New York, Simon and Schuster, 1954.

INDEX

A

Adjective Check List, 12, 17, 18, 21, 24, 25, and individual cases
Alcoholism, 12, 19, 37, 45, 49
Ambisexuality, 68
Ambivalence, 9
American Psychiatric Association, 66, 74
Anxiety, 9, 13, 25, 36, 47, 48, 49, 52, 60, 65, 72
Armon, V., 10, 13, 66, 70
Asimos, C., 65
Auerback, A. E., 65, 72

B

Bacon, C. L., 7
Beach, F. A., 3
Bene, E., 11
Bergler, E., 7
Bisexuality, 3, 6, 12, 20, 21, 35, 36, 45, 66, 68
British Medical Association, 70, 74

C

Caprio, F. S., 7, 13
Castration complex, 6, 7
Causation. (see Female homosexuality, etiology of)
Center for Special Problems, 72
Children of lesbian mothers, 74-75
Civil rights of lesbians, 69n
Clitoral fixation, 8
Conditioning, 10
Constitutional factors, 8, 8n, 10
Cory, D. W., 8, 10, 66, 75
"Crushes", 9, 40, 42, 43
"Cure" of female homosexuality, 5, 67, 72

D

Daughters of Bilitis, 17, 18, 22
DaVinci, Leonardo, 66

Defense mechanisms, 9
Definition of female homosexuality, 17
Dependency, 8, 11, 13
Depression, 12, 13, 65, 72
de Saussure, R., 6
Deutsch, H., 6, 7

E

Endocrine factors, 8, 8n
Etiology of female homosexuality. (see Female homosexuality, etiology of)

F

Family Adjustment Test, 13
Family patterns of sexual adjustment, 10, 20, 29, and individual cases
Father, dominant, 12, 29
Father-fixation, 6
Female homosexuality
  as defense, 11, 71
  as illness, 65
  as learned condition, 8, 66
  as sexual variance, 10, 66
  as way of life, 17, 66-67
  attitudes of society toward, 5, 11, 68, 72
  bisexuality in, 12, 20, and cases A, B, K, O
  characteristics of relationships in, 7, 9, 15, 17, 22-23, 25
  defined, 17
  "early prodromata" of, 9
  emotional instability in, 11, 65, 72, 74
  "escape" into, 7, 9
  etiology of, 5-11, 29, 63, 70-73
  mental health in, 11, 12, 13, 65, 73, 74
  neurotic traits in, 11, 12, 13, 65
  not a clinical entity, 11, 66
  psychiatric classification of, 74
  psychological characteristics of com-